The TM Technique

A Skeptics Guide to the TM Program

D1264117

A SKEPTIC'S
GUIDE TO THE
TM PROGRAM

THE TM TECHNIQUE

PETER RUSSELL

D

$ 3.95

The TM Technique

A Skeptics Guide to the TM Program

Peter Russell

Routledge & Kegan Paul

Boston, London and Henley

First published in 1976
by Routledge & Kegan Paul
9 Park Street,
Boston, Mass. 02108, USA
under the title *The TM Technique*

Reprinted and first published as a paperback 1977
and printed in the USA
© Peter Russell 1976, 1977

ISBN 0 7100 8672 5

Contents

Contents

Introduction

Towards the end of 1967 I was browsing through the shelves of my local library when I came across a book entitled *The Science of Being and Art of Living* by Maharishi Mahesh Yogi. Having a growing interest in various forms of meditation, I added the book to the half dozen others I had picked out and carried on browsing down the shelves.

It was some days before I got round to opening Maharishi's book, but when I did I was taken by surprise. Throughout the book he was saying the exact opposite of everything I had read about meditation, and even appeared to be contradicting the 'authorities' in the field. Meditation, he said, could be easy; it did not require effort or control; anyone could meditate whatever their disposition or life-style. He was turning most of the traditional teachings upside down: yet he seemed to make a lot more sense than many of the other teachers I had come across. Having studied the book at length I decided that if the Transcendental Meditation (TM) technique itself was even half as remarkable as his book then I must try it.

My initial experience was not, I must admit, all that I had hoped for, but this, I soon realized, was not the fault of the technique: the error lay in my being too analytical about the process. At this stage my academic training was more of a hindrance than a help. Over the next few months, however, the long-term effects of meditation started to become noticeable. I was feeling much calmer, more stable, more self-assured, and getting things done more quickly and more effectively. At the same time several friends who had initially watched my venture with some caution, and perhaps a little amusement, decided that they too would like to try it, and I found my own experiences being confirmed by the changes I observed in others.

My appreciation of the TM program grew steadily, and when in 1969 I had the chance of taking a year to myself I decided to travel to India to study the field further. It was obvious that if I was to go deeper into the subject I needed to spend some time at the source of the teaching. My trip was well rewarded: both my experience and understanding of the field increased beyond all measure and before leaving India I decided to train as a TM instructor. In the five years since then I have been researching further into the TM program. This, together with the experience of teaching the technique to several hundred others, has convinced me that here is a most valuable, although largely misunderstood, practice.

The popular image of meditation generally has been one of something a little mystical and not really suited to us living in the West in the twentieth century. This is to some extent understandable. Meditation has generally been associated with a withdrawn monastic life-style and thought to be of interest only to the spiritually inclined. But this is not because meditation is itself an inherently reclusive practice. Teachings such as Maharishi's have always been formulated in the language of the times. If today meditation is thought to be something of an anachronism and of little relevance to a scientific-technological society it is only because it has not yet been formulated in the language of the present day. Maharishi is putting the theory and practice of meditation into a twentieth-century context and showing that far from being a vague metaphysical ideal it is a practical teaching which can be investigated and understood in terms of physiology, psychology, sociology, etc. He is proving that it is just as valuable – if not more valuable – today as it ever was. And for just this reason it is even more important that the subject be given a contemporary formulation.

Many people are naturally very skeptical about the claims made by the TM movement, and for a while I was very much a skeptic myself. The claims made for the TM program are far-reaching and often contrary to popular belief. Only the naïve, I felt, could be anything but skeptical. Gradually, however, many of my doubts have been resolved. On a practical level, my own experiences of the TM program, and those of many others I have instructed, showed me that much of what Maharishi was claiming was true. And on a theoretical level, I have, over the years, had to consider the numerous queries and doubts raised by other skeptics, and have found that the deeper I examine the subject the more valid it becomes. In this book I have tried to go into many of the questions commonly raised about the TM technique and its effects, and give the reader a deeper understanding of what the TM technique is and is not. As such I trust it will be of value to both meditator and non-meditator alike.

In view of my personal interest in the TM technique one might wonder whether I was not biased towards the subject. Certainly I have come to regard it as a most valuable technique – indeed, if I did not believe it was of such value I would hardly be so willing to sit down for a year and write a book about it – but I challenge any suggestion that my personal involvement prevents me from writing as fair an account of the subject as someone who is looking at it from the outside. On the contrary, the person who has not spent some time acquainting himself with both the technique and the teachings behind it is hardly in a good position to present a comprehensive account of the subject.

The TM program validated itself to me not through critical analysis but through personal experience supported by the experiences of others I have taught; by Maharishi's writings and lectures on the subject; by a comparison with similar teachings which have arisen in most cultures at one time or another; by a consideration of the TM program in the light of contemporary physiology, psychology and physics; and by the recent experimental studies of the subject. In this book I have tried to bring these various approaches together in the belief that by throwing light upon the subject from as many different angles as possible the general reader may more readily gain a comprehensive vision of the TM technique and its effects.

The specialist may feel some dissatisfaction when his or her own subject has not been dealt with as adequately as they would wish.

This is inevitable with a book which takes a general, multi-disciplinary approach. I must however emphasize that none of the various approaches is meant to prove that the TM technique works: they are merely different windows into the subject.

Although I have in many instances drawn upon similar teachings from other cultures and other ages in order to illustrate particular points I have not attempted to make a comparative study of the TM program with respect to other self-development programs. Such a comparative study may well be due; but if so it must be based upon a clear understanding of what the TM technique is and how it works. Many articles have appeared in the popular press comparing the TM program to other programs, but very often they have only revealed a profound lack of any real understanding of the TM technique itself. I hope that by laying down a fairly comprehensive picture of the TM program and its effects future analyses may at least be based on a reasonably faithful understanding of the subject – though ideally they should be based on a clear personal experience of the subject as well.

The TM program is applicable equally to men and women and wherever possible I have tried to remove the sexist implications inherent in our language. In some cases, though, this would have involved some cumbersome phrasing and in these instances I have used the words 'he' and 'his' with the expanded meanings of 'he' or 'she', and 'his' or 'her(s)'.

Finally a word on the use of analogies. Throughout history teachers of meditation have made liberal use of analogies and parables, and Maharishi is no exception. The ideas being put forward are often very foreign to our own way of thinking and, by likening the situation to a more familiar experience, an abstract point can be made more concrete and the pupil given a better idea of what the teacher is trying to say. The various analogies used in this book are not therefore meant to prove any points; only to relate the points to everyday experience. One must also remember that an analogy is only a similarity: as much as it is like the situation under consideration it is also unlike it, and any analogy will, if taken too far, break down.

Acknowledgments

My indebtedness to Maharishi Mahesh Yogi for his knowledge and inspiration goes without saying.

I also owe much to Dr John Allison whose personal guidance in the practice and theory of the TM technique laid a firm foundation to my interest in the subject.

With regard to the production of this book I would like to thank Charmian Campbell and Dr Ivor Pleydell-Pearce who both managed to struggle through and comment upon my rather untidy first draft; Chris Robertson for being a continual source of feedback, discussing at length with me many of the finer arguments and pointing out several interesting cross-connections which I would otherwise have missed; and Dr Diana Surman for helping to tidy up my rather cumbersome use of the English language. I would also like to thank Marion Fisken, Phil and Harriet Jump, Gill Robertson, and Penny and Philip Townsend, each of whom helped in more material and domestic matters at various stages of the book's preparation.

Part One

This book falls naturally into three parts. The first part deals mainly with the Transcendental Meditation technique itself. Chapter 1 starts with a brief introduction to the subject, explaining the technique, its role in life, and how it is taught. This is followed in Chapter 2 by a look at the origins and history of the practice, and how it is spreading through the world today. Chapter 3 is more theoretical and looks at Maharishi's description of the human thinking process and the principles which underlie the TM technique, and Chapter 4 describes how the technique works. The last three chapters of this section deal with the effects of the TM technique upon the individual. In Chapter 5 some of the scientific research into the TM program is reviewed, looking particularly at the state of rest which results in both the body and the brain. Chapter 6 shows how this deep rest dissolves accumulated stresses and Chapter 7 considers the all-round improvement in the quality of life which such relief from stress brings.

Part Two goes on to look at the changes in awareness of both oneself and the world around which come with the regular practice of the TM technique, and Part Three considers the implications of such changes for society as a whole.

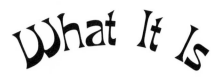

What It Is

1

Every minute of the day someone new learns the Transcendental Meditation technique. He or she may be a doctor, a teacher, an artist, a labourer, a business executive, a housewife, a policeman, a student, a politician, a university professor, or someone from any other walk of life. What is it they are all learning to do and why?

The Transcendental Meditation technique (or the TM technique, as it is commonly abbreviated) allows the mind to settle down to a less excited state. The person experiences quieter and quieter levels of thinking till he or she arrives at a state of complete mental stillness. In this state the attention is said to have gone beyond, or transcended, the everyday levels of thought – hence the description 'Transcendental Meditation'.

As the mind settles down the body follows suit, becoming more relaxed than during sleep. One does not however go to sleep: one remains fully conscious and is usually aware of all that is happening in the world around. It is not a state of unconsciousness or hypnotic trance: it is simply a state of mental and physical quiet along with full inner wakefulness.

To practise the TM technique takes about twenty minutes twice a day, once in the morning and again in the early evening. One simply sits down comfortably, closes the eyes and begins the mental practice. As a result the mind is allowed to settle down into a state of complete rest.

Now notice that I said 'as a *result* the mind is *allowed* to settle down . . .'. This is very important. In the TM technique there is no attempt to force the mind to settle down; once started the process happens of its own accord without any control or coercion on the part of the individual – indeed, any such attempt would almost certainly disturb the process. This complete lack of effort and control distinguishes the TM technique from most other techniques of relaxation and meditation.

The word 'meditation' covers a wide range of techniques with many different associations. For some the word may imply holding the mind to some mental image, or possibly to the idea of nothing; to others it may mean speculating on some chosen theme, or meticulously examining the contents of one's mind. Since all these meanings and many more have, at one time or another, passed under the umbrella of 'meditation' it is often presumed that the Transcendental Meditation technique must involve one or other of these practices. But this is not the case. As we shall see in Chapter 4 it is unlike any of these concepts of 'meditation'. In fact the word 'meditation' is probably something of a misnomer as far as the TM technique is concerned. But there is no other word in the English language which seems adequately to describe the practice without being equally ambivalent and misleading, so we shall have to accept it as the most approximate description of the technique.

Unlike some other forms of meditation the TM program does not advocate any renunciation of worldly affairs. The actual practice of meditation, it is true, does involve a temporary withdrawal from activity, but it is a withdrawal in order that one may return to activity that much more effectively. It is a recharging of one's mental and physical resources and on returning to their daily tasks meditators find they have far greater energy and efficiency. Rather than being a withdrawal from the world the TM technique is a balancing of the intense activity to which most of us are fully committed by a corresponding degree of profound rest. Rather than reducing activity, the TM technique enhances it.

The basic Transcendental Meditation technique is the same for everyone. The process is not concerned with the meaning of thoughts but with the way thoughts develop in the mind. And whether a person be an artist or scientist, young or old, English or Indian, the way their thoughts develop is essentially the same, and their TM practice is essentially the same.

The technique does not involve sitting in any strange physical postures, any change of life-style, or the adoption of any philosophy. There is, as will become apparent later, a large body of theory which complements the TM technique and which may well be regarded as a philosophy, but it is not necessary to accept this in order for the practice to have its effects. Being independent of what you are thinking *about*, the TM technique is not affected by your own personal beliefs. Indeed you do not even have to believe that it will work; providing you follow the correct practice the effects follow automatically.

Until a few years ago science had regarded meditation as a very subjective affair and had had very little to say about it. But now that states of consciousness are becoming of increasing importance in many fields of science, and recent developments in physiology and psychology have made it possible to study in some detail the effects of meditation, the subject is rapidly gaining respectability. Since 1970 there has been considerable research into the effects of the TM technique and many of the claims of meditators have been confirmed. Physiologists have shown that the technique does indeed produce a state of profound rest and relief from stress, and psychologists have found that afterwards people are more peaceful, relaxed and efficient. This scientific support has led to a marked reduction in the skepticism which initially surrounded the TM program.

Dissolving Stress

Another factor which has contributed to the rapid expansion of the TM movement over the last few years is its effectiveness in reducing stress. Technological advances and large-scale indus-trialization may have relieved us of many of our physical burdens and helped increase our material standards of living but in their wake has come a significant increase in our mental burdens. It is this mental load which we commonly refer to as stress.

The actual sources of stress are numerous. Walking down a city street, driving in traffic, working amidst the din of factory machinery, living near a busy airport, struggling through the rush hour and having to deal with other tense people are all common causes of stress. Increased competition and insecurity result in so much tension and anxiety that 'mental breakdowns' and heart diseases have become more or less an occupational hazard in many professions. The more demanding the job the greater the stress. Air traffic controllers, for instance, who may each be responsible for the safety of a hundred lives once a minute show one of the highest incidences of peptic ulcers. At the other end of the spectrum the boredom and monotony of a production line can have similar effects.

The rapidly accelerating pace of modern life means that we are meeting new situations, making new decisions, and even changing life-styles faster and faster. The body has to adapt and readapt to each new change, and when the environment starts changing faster than the body can adapt we begin to accumulate stress. The faster the changes come the more stress is accumulated. The pressure is now becoming so great that normal sleep no longer gives the body sufficient chance to recover from the overload and many people end up permanently stressed and tense.

Today it is no longer infectious diseases which are the major killers but 'stress diseases'. Many doctors now believe that over 75 per cent of our illnesses have their roots in stress and over 50 per cent of all deaths are from stress-related disorders. U.S. doctors write over 250,000,000 prescriptions a year for tranquillizers and anti-depressants. On top of this there are the many other drugs such as aspirin which are bought over the counter, and ten thousand million dollars spent each year on cigarettes. But suppressing the symptoms, which is essentially what this approach is doing, does not remove the stress and sooner or later it will reappear in some other form. Moreover, as well as depressing the physiological excitement most drugs also depress the person's sensitivity and alertness as well.

What then is the solution? The pressures in the world are there and they're not going to disappear in the foreseeable future. It is not, however, the pressures themselves which are the trouble so much as our inability to cope with them. The increasing pace of life is demanding that we take extra rest to balance the extra pressures yet at the same time it is itself prohibiting us from taking this rest. What we need is a more intense form of daily rest.

Indeed, if the body is not given this rest it eventually falls ill forcing us to take extra rest – or at least it makes abundantly clear that it needs more rest. If we continue to ignore its natural needs

then we may find ourselves heading for a rest of a more permanent nature.

The question is how to relax. It is not always as easy as it
sounds. It is very easy to raise your blood pressure. Just to think
of a frightening experience will do it for you immediately. But you
cannot lower it as quickly by simply thinking of a soothing
experience. Paradoxically the more tense a person is the harder it
is to relax. The anxious person is prone to *try* to relax and
becomes even more anxious on finding that he or she cannot. It is
here that the TM technique is so beneficial. Firstly, there is no
deliberate attempt to relax, the whole process happens quite
automatically. And secondly, the practice can be comfortably
integrated into a normal daily routine and so neutralize stresses
and tension as they arise.

Physiological research indicates that the TM process is the exact
opposite of that by which the body accumulates stress. Whereas
stress results in a bigger heart rate, increased breathing, raised
blood pressure and general physiological excitement; the TM
technique produces a slower heart rate, decreased breathing, lower
blood pressure and general relaxation. By giving the body and
mind two periods of additional deep rest, twice a day, the TM
technique neutralizes tensions as they are incurred and simultaneously dissolves the many accumulated stresses that were
untouched by normal sleep. Moreover, it does this without
decreasing mental alertness or sensitivity. The effect is very much
as if one had fitted the rest and refreshment of a weekend into just
twenty minutes.

Having this much rest twice a day instead of just once a week
leads not only to an all-round improvement in health, but to a
greater clarity of thought, a much better use of personal resources,
more efficient action, and a greater resilience to further stress. In
short the whole of life becomes more enjoyable, rewarding and
fulfilling.

The TM Program

The basic instruction in the TM technique is very simple. It is
usually taught in four lessons over four consecutive days, each
lesson lasting between one and one and a half hours. The instruction is carried out by qualified TM teachers, of whom there
are now over ten thousand throughout the world, and weekly

courses are available at most of the thousand or so teaching centers which have been established (see Appendix).

The teaching has been standardized so that the procedure is the same no matter who the teacher or what the country, and takes place in seven steps.

The first step is an introductory lecture which gives 'a vision of possibilities' offered by the TM program. It is concerned primarily with the benefits which the person who starts the course is likely to experience, and with a very general understanding of the basic principles on which the technique is based. This is followed by a 'Preparatory Talk' which deals more with the theory of meditation, and covers all that it is necessary for a person to know before starting the practice.

After the Preparatory Talk those wishing to start the TM technique have a short private interview with their teacher. This is in order that both may get to know each other a little and deal with any personal queries.

The fourth step is one of personal instruction in the technique and takes about one hour. The fifth, sixth and seventh steps are for 'verification and validation of experiences'. During these days one practises at home twice a day and receives additional instruction and explanation during the teaching periods. These next three sessions are usually given in groups, so that one may also gain from the experience of others, although there is always the opportunity of private consultations with the teacher.

After these four days of instruction most people are well established in the technique and continue the practice without any trouble. But although very simple the TM technique is also very delicate, and the new meditator may unintentionally introduce some slight modification into the practice, with the result that it is no longer so effective, and probably not so enjoyable. In order to catch any such intrusions at an early stage it is important that the new TM student returns to a teacher periodically for what is called 'checking'. In the beginning this may mean meeting with the teacher once a fortnight, or once a month. Later it is reduced to about once every few months. As well as keeping the technique of meditation in trim, these meetings also give the individual a chance to understand more about his experiences and personal development.

Origins and Growth

2

The Transcendental Meditation technique is not new: it has a long and distinguished history stretching back several thousand years. It may not have always had the same name but the same basic technique has been taught many times in the past. But although the TM technique may have been known and taught before, its history has not been a continuous one. The knowledge has been lost many times.

This loss is the inevitable consequence of the teaching becoming slightly distorted each time it is passed on from one person to another. When this happens time after time the teachings become so diluted and shrouded in misunderstanding that very little of the original remains. It is rather like taking a photocopy of a photocopy of a photocopy of a . . . , each copy becomes a little more distorted and unintelligible until finally the original has disappeared.

As the practices become distorted they rapidly lose their effectiveness and no longer work so well. They are then, quite naturally, cast aside and all that remains are the empty verbal descriptions of meditation and its effects. Any further suggestion that meditation could in fact be easy is inevitably treated with scorn.

Although the practices may become lost to the world at large the seeds from which the teachings originally sprang live on and from time to time some teacher comes and tries to spread the original techniques once again. Today we are witnessing such a revival of this ancient teaching, and one which is spreading right across the world. The teacher who at this time has brought the technique out to the world is Maharishi Mahesh Yogi, commonly known as just Maharishi.

Brahmananda Saraswati

Before Maharishi came out of the Himalayas in 1955, he had been a devoted disciple of the renowned Indian sage Brahmananda Saraswati. His full title was Swami Brahmananda Saraswati, Maharaj, Jagat-Guru Bhagwan Shankaracharya of Jyotir-Math, but he is referred to by Maharishi as simply 'Guru Dev'. This is a common title in India and is used to refer to the master who leads a tradition. It can be simply translated as 'Divine Teacher'.

Guru Dev was born in 1868 and started his spiritual quest at the early age of nine. As a small boy he felt that there was no lasting satisfaction to be gained from worldly 'pleasures' and that true fulfilment came from within. So he set off in search of a spiritual master. He travelled up to the Himalayas where he searched for four years before coming across a teacher who satisfied his high criteria: not only had he to be learned in philosophy but also an enlightened man and a lifelong celibate.

Although Maharishi rarely talks of his master's life, maintaining that incidents from his outer life can never do justice to such a man's true significance (his inner state of consciousness), he does nevertheless tell one story which illustrates the strict care which the young boy took in his search for a master.

During his travels the boy came across a certain sannyasin who was purported to be an 'enlightened man'. A sannyasin is a recluse and one who has renounced all material possessions and worldly pleasures. By tradition such people are not allowed to cook their own food for it is part of their austerity that they do not use fire. When the boy met the sannyasin the first thing he did was to ask if he might have some fire. The man immediately became angered and reprimanded the child for having asked such a thing: didn't he know that sannyasins never had any fire and that it was a great insult to request such a thing? The boy simply replied that if he had no fire from where had it flared up? The man calmed down and recognizing that this was more than a simple child standing before him entreated the boy to stay and become his disciple. But the boy had seen enough to know that this 'saint' failed to meet his requirements.

After four years of searching through the Himalayas he eventually came across a man who satisfied his requirements. This was Swami Shri Krishanand Saraswati, a great sage of the time, who lived deep in the mountains at a place called Uttar Kashi, often called 'The Valley of the Saints'. The boy soon became his closest disciple and remained with him for twenty years.

At the age of thirty-four he left his master's side and retired to a cave in central India to live in solitude for forty years. He was almost completely cut off from any other people, these mountains being some of the thickest and wildest in India, yet even from the little contact that he did have with others he became widely renowned as an enlightened man.

After twenty years of solitude he was requested to leave the mountains and take up the chair of Shankaracharya of Jyotir-Math in northern India. This was one of the four seats of learning that Shankara had set up many centuries before in an attempt to preserve his teaching from distortion, but for the last hundred and fifty years no one had been found worthy enough of this position. It was clear to the custodians of Shankara's tradition that Brahmananda Saraswati was a fully realized man and one who could lead the people of India back to the original teachings, and they asked him to take up the chair. But he refused. Repeatedly messages were sent to him urging him to come out of the forest and fill this important position but just as consistently he refused. It was to be another twenty years before he finally took the position.

Every twelve years in India there is a large gathering of 'saints' and holy men at Allahabad where two of the holy rivers, the Ganges and the Yamuna, meet. This festival is called the Kumbla Mela and it is customary for many of the recluses to come down from the mountains for this occasion. Along with thousands of others Guru Dev had left his cave to attend. Making the best of the opportunity his proponents finally persuaded him to accept the position of Shankaracharya.

Guru Dev did not return to the mountains but spent the rest of his life travelling and teaching throughout northern India trying to re-establish a correct understanding of the ancient teachings. Although little known in the West he became revered by many in India as a perfect example of a fully enlightened being. Dr Radhakrishnan, the famous Indian philosopher, hailed him as 'Vedanta Incarnate' – the embodiment of the highest Indian wisdom.

Maharishi and the Growth of the TM Movement

At this time Maharishi was studying physics and chemistry at Allahabad University. Besides his studies he also maintained a lively interest in spiritual teachers, and on hearing that Brahmananda Saraswati was in Allahabad for a while he went along one evening to the house where he was staying.

Maharishi relates how he had been quietly ushered on to the flat roof of the house and was sitting there in darkness and silence unable to see or hear anything of this renowned saint. After some time a car swung round in the distance and the beam from the headlights momentarily caught the sage's face. Immediately, without having spoken to him, Maharishi saw that here was a profoundly serene and wise individual. After several more visits he decided to become a disciple of this man. Guru Dev accepted him, but on the condition that he first went back to finish his studies. This Maharishi did, then returned and spent the next twelve years studying, learning and working with Guru Dev.

During this time Maharishi had become Guru Dev's closest disciple and at his master's death inherited all the knowledge of his tradition. With this knowledge he retired to an isolated cave deep in the Himalayas. But after two years of silence he gradually felt drawn back out into the world. At first he resisted the idea, it being the thought by the recluses of that area that the outside world was like mud, and that there could be no reason why an enlightened man should want to go out and dirty himself. Maharishi's feeling, though, grew stronger and stronger, and eventually he left the peace and solitude of his mountain cave and came down to the plains of northern India. From there he travelled on until he came to a town in the state of Kerala in the South of India.

He had made no specific plans to talk there, he had simply been drawn to visit the place, but within a couple of days after his arrival he was approached by a man who, recognizing him as a monk from the north, asked him to give a week of lectures. Maharishi accepted and the popularity of his first lectures was such that by the seventh talk the hall that had been hired was overfilled. He was immediately asked to speak in other towns around the area and ended up spending the next six months lecturing and teaching the TM technique throughout the state.

Since then Maharishi's two years of silence have been followed by nearly twenty years of the most intense activity. Maharishi works continually, morning, afternoon, evening, and far into the night, day after day and month after month. He has no time to engage in idle gossip or read newspapers; every minute is devoted to the task of spreading the TM technique as effectively and quickly as possible.

But in spite of the time and effort he pours into his work Maharishi never takes any personal credit for his successes. If ever any credit is due it always goes to his master, Guru Dev. For this reason he will always be heard to end any lecture or discussion with the phrase 'Jai Guru Dev', meaning simply 'By the grace of Guru Dev'. With this expression he is acknowledging that it is only through Guru Dev that the teaching has been made available again today.

After leaving Kerala he spent two years travelling and teaching around India, rapidly gaining acceptance both for himself as a teacher and for the TM technique. In 1958 he established the Spiritual Regeneration Movement (SRM) in Madras laying a more permanent foundation to his movement and set off to take his message further afield.

He argued that one reason why many Western nations were more prosperous than India was because they were more open to accepting change; they were able freely to try out and take up new ideas. So if he was to succeed in getting the world interested in the Transcendental Meditation program he must go to the more 'progressive' nations first. In 1958 he left India and travelling east through Singapore and Hawaii arrived in California early in 1959. He stayed there for several months teaching the TM technique and establishing a permanent national center for the SRM, then went on eastwards to New York and Europe.

By the end of one year so many people were wanting to learn the technique that Maharishi realized he could no longer personally cope with the demand. So he decided to embark upon the training of TM teachers. This decision represented a radical

change in the Indian tradition. Previously the teaching of meditation had always been undertaken by the master of the tradition,
or by his closer disciples, but Maharishi was taking ordinary
Westerners and training them to teach meditation. This does not
mean that he was creating Western gurus or spiritual masters: he
was simply instructing people in the art of teaching the TM
technique and this can be done by most people who have had
some personal experience of the practice and who have undergone
the appropriate training.

Initially this training took place in India near Rishikesh, a little
town situated at the point where the Ganges emerges from the
Himalayas, and the start of a major pilgrimage for many Indians.
Just outside the town, a little way up the wooded and sharply
rising slopes, Maharishi had built an academy of meditation. Here
would-be teachers spent three months learning the art of teaching
the TM technique.

The first courses consisted of about thirty participants but by
1970 they had expanded to two hundred. Faced with an ever-
increasing demand for teachers he moved the courses to Europe
and set up facilities for training a thousand or more teachers at a
time. More recently he has extended the teacher training course so
that the first stage of the training can be completed at home. By
1977 he had trained over ten thousand teachers of the TM
program.

When Maharishi first came to the West he found that many
people were a little wary of anything 'spiritual' and were often put
off by the name of his organization, i.e. The Spiritual Regeneration Movement. So in 1960 he founded the more neutral sounding
'International Meditation Society' (IMS), and in 1965 the
'Student's International Meditation Society' (SIMS) to cope with
the rapidly increasing demand for TM instruction amongst the
student population and others of that age-group.

The initial rapid growth of interest among students is probably
accounted for by the increasing disillusionment with the 'consumer society' and conventional education, and the realization
that the drug experience did not appear to be providing the
anticipated 'alternative consciousness'. At the same time scientists
in the West began to take a greater interest in the physiological
and psychological effects of meditation, and as a result the TM
program has gained in respectability. This has led to the establishment of two more organizations: the Maharishi Interna-

tional University (MIU), which is integrating the study of the TM program with conventional academic disciplines (see Chapter 14), and the Foundation for the Science of Creative Intelligence which is primarily concerned with introducing the benefits of the TM program to business and industry. Over the last ten years the TM movement in America has enjoyed a steady annual growth rate of around 100 per cent – which makes it one of the fastest growing organizations in the world. By mid-1975 there were 550,000 people who had learnt the TM technique in America and more than a million across the world, and the figure was growing at the rate of 35,000 per month.

The rapid growth of interest in the TM program has not been confined to America and Europe. With the present exception of Russia and China, the TM technique is being taught in almost every country of the world. Some of the greatest interest has been shown by India itself to which the technique has now returned wearing the clothes of the West.

But whatever its packaging the teaching always remains the same. The different styles of presentation which Maharishi has created are just different ways of putting the same message across to different audiences. And, just as apples will continue to fall whether you think that the reason lies in the apple's tendency to fall, the force of gravity, or the curvature of space-time, so the TM technique will have the same effects on the mind and body whether you understand the process in terms of the release of stress, the development of Creative Intelligence, or the expansion of consciousness.

Maintaining the Purity of the Teaching

With many other meditation practices and systems of self-development one finds that the benefits and rewards described by the teacher bear little or no relation to the concerns of the man-in-the-street. The listener is often left puzzled and confused, if not highly incredulous. Maharishi, however, is always at great pains to ensure that his pupils are receiving the teaching on a level they can relate to and comprehend.

Having received a university education in science Maharishi is able to combine a logical systematic approach to knowledge with a personal awareness of the full range of higher states of consciousness. This combination has been of enormous benefit in

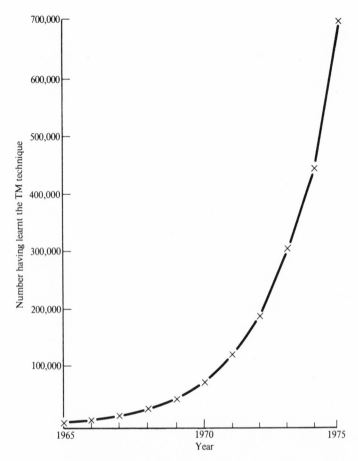

Figure 1   *The growth of the TM movement in the United States (Data supplied by SIMS National HQ, Los Angeles). The growth in other countries has followed a similar exponential pattern although involving smaller numbers. (An extrapolation of this curve shows the whole of the US having learnt the TM technique by 1983. This state of affairs is unlikely to come about quite so rapidly because exponential growth rates only occur when the growing group is small compared with the total population. As the proportion of people practising the technique becomes a sizeable proportion of the total population the curve will tend to flatten out.)*

allowing him to put this ancient wisdom to western people in terms which they can understand, and has undoubtedly contributed to the rapid acceptance of his teaching.

Inseparable from his desire to bring the TM technique to the world is his aim to keep the teaching as pure as possible. He wants to ensure that this present revival of the tradition is not distorted and lost as rapidly as it has been in the past. Eventually, of course, it will suffer the same fate but Maharishi is trying to take steps to ensure that this loss occurs as slowly as possible.

Every lecture he gives is being recorded, all on audio- and most on video-tape, in order to provide a more permanent and faithful record of what he has said. This is the first time in history that it has been possible to preserve such a teaching so faithfully and hopefully this will help it retain its purity for much longer.

But one must also ensure that the individuals who are practising the TM technique do not themselves distort it. Although the practice is simple and easy it is also very delicate and the novice may inadvertently distort the technique a little before he or she has grasped it completely. This invariably leads to some control or restraint being introduced and the practice which has been modified in this way is seldom so effective. In order to prevent this Maharishi always advises frequent 'checking' in the first few months of the practice and also insists that one does not deliberately mix the TM technique with any other technique. This is not necessarily because the other practices are in themselves of no value, only that the TM technique is complete in itself. Any attempt to add to the technique invariably turns out to be a subtraction.

From my own experience of TM instruction I have found that when occasionally people complain that the technique is no longer working satisfactorily it is often because they have unconsciously modified the practice a little. In effect they are no longer practising the TM technique but something slightly different. It is not that the TM technique is no longer working but that the modified practice is not so effective.

As well as not mixing up the TM technique with other practices, Maharishi insists that TM theory be kept separate from various philosophies or metaphysical systems. Again this is not because other points of view are necessarily wrong, within their own frame of reference they may well be perfectly valid, but because they will usually muddle one's understanding of the TM process. The slightest turn away from the correct teaching may not seem very significant today but in a generation or so that innocuous seed could have grown up to become the source of considerable misunderstanding and distortion of the practice.

Maharishi is also effecting a fundamental change in the mode of propagation of the teaching. In the past it was virtually impossible to prevent distortion creeping in. In the absence of 'mass media', telecommunications or air travel, the only way in which a teaching could be spread was by personally handing it on. Maharishi has tried to eliminate this treacherous process of dissemination by effectively bringing everyone who learns the TM technique back to the source so that they have the practice first hand. It is obviously impossible for everyone to learn the technique personally from Maharishi, nevertheless it has been possible for him personally to train enough teachers. Only when Maharishi is satisfied that the student has fully grasped the fundamentals of this teaching will he permit him or her to go out and teach other people. In this way he is ensuring that every TM teacher has the knowledge in its purity and that every TM student is effectively coming back to the source to receive the practice in its purity.

The Nature of the Mind

3

Maharishi's teachings are notably different from many of the others which have emerged from India and the East in that he never belittles the material side of life or the importance of physical well-being. Other teachers can be found claiming that spiritual or inner development should be one's prime or even sole ambition. Some go so far as to deny the reality of the physical world, relegating it to the realm of illusion to be ignored or even rejected. Maharishi, however, will have none of this. He continually emphasizes the reality of the world around us, the importance of physical well-being, and the intimate interdependence of the physical and the mental.

It is a basic premise of modern psychology that for every mental change, for every thought, experience, desire and feeling, there is a corresponding activity or change in the brain. It is now being recognized that the converse is also true: that for every physiological change and activity in the brain there is a corresponding change in mental activity; that *everything* that happens inside our brains affects our mental state in some way or other. Most of these mental changes pass unnoticed, only the strongest changes being consciously appreciated.

'A thought,' writes Maharishi, 'starts from the deepest level of consciousness and rises through the whole depth ... of the mind until it finally appears as a conscious thought at the surface.' He illustrates this with an analogy of a bubble rising in a pond. If the pond is murky then all that we see is the bubble bursting on the surface. We do not see it starting from the bottom of the pond and travelling up to meet the surface. Similarly, because our minds are dull, the rising, or development, of a thought in the mind is hidden from 'view'. 'Thus,' he continues, 'we find that every thought stirs the whole range of the depth of consciousness but is appreciated only when it reaches the conscious level; its earlier stages are not appreciated.'[1]

This image of a thought rising in the mind is, of course, only a model and must not be taken too literally. It is nevertheless an instructive and useful model, and there is considerable evidence that analogous processes may be taking place in the brain.

Several different lines of research suggest that it takes about a tenth of a second for the brain to generate a conscious experience. Now a tenth of a second might seem a very brief time but by neurological standards it is pretty long. When we consider that one neuron is able to excite another in about one thousandth of a second and that each neuron may interact with a thousand or more others it rapidly becomes apparent that an immensely complex activity can be established in one tenth of a second: complex not only in the sense of there being many neurons involved but also in the sense of being highly organized and structured.

If we are to become aware of one specific neural activity, a visual event say, then that activity must somehow be distinguished from the vast amount of other activity that is going on in the brain. It is probable that the distinguishing factor is organization. Those neural processes which give rise to conscious experiences are those which possess a greater degree of order and structure. Indeed, there is a good case to be made for the view that conscious experience is the mental counterpart of organization on the physical level; that consciousness is the complement of a highly structured nervous system, and that specific mental experiences are the complementary aspects of coherent activity within the nervous system.[2] Sir John Eccles, the celebrated neurophysiologist, has remarked that the activity of the human brain is the most complex process in the entire solar system. It should, therefore, also be the most conscious process in the solar system.

A mathematical analysis of the situation suggests that it is only necessary for a very small percentage (0.001 per cent) of the neurons throughout the brain to be coherent in order that a neural activity be distinguishable from the less coherent background activity. It is likely that it is this ordering of a small percentage of the neurons which occurs in the tenth of a second taken to generate a thought.

In cybernetic terms the process of organization increases the signal-to-noise ratio. The signal is the experience being attended to and the noise is all the other unwanted activity. By increasing the coherence of the 'desired' information it is differentiated more clearly from all the background noise and therefore gives rise to a stronger conscious experience.

The actual degree of coherence necessary for a thought to break through into consciousness will depend upon the level of the background activity. There is in effect a threshold for conscious experience. Activities with a relatively poor degree of coherence remain subliminal (literally, below the threshold), masked out by other more coherent activities; activities with sufficient coherence just to pass the threshold will give rise to dim, hazy thoughts; while more strongly ordered activities will be appreciated as clear conscious experiences.

The parallels with Maharishi's model of the mind are fairly obvious. The rising of the 'thought bubble' corresponds to the progressive complexification and organization of the neural signals in the brain. The thought gets stronger and stronger as the coherence increases until it breaks through above the surrounding mental 'noise' to be appreciated as a thought on 'the conscious level of the mind'.

Figure 2 illustrates Maharishi's description of the process. The same diagram could equally well be used to illustrate the concurrent processes in the brain and so I have added to Maharishi's labelling a parallel physical one.

The Source of Thought

Every thought starts from the deepest levels of the mind as the faintest impulse and as it rises towards the surface it begins to gain structure. The structure of a thought determines its meaning and the meaning distinguishes one thought from another. At the moment of their inception all thoughts are qualityless and indis-

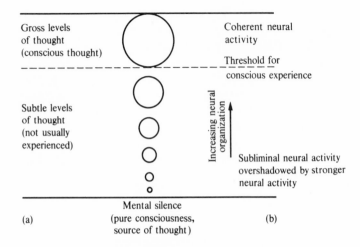

Figure 2   *The 'rising' of a thought in the mind.*
           (a) Maharishi's description of process.
           (b) Possible physical counterpart.

tinguishable one from another, but as they rise towards consciousness they each become more specific and more differentiated from other possible thoughts until, on arriving at the gross conscious levels of everyday thinking, each thought is a unique, clearly defined, experience.

If we were to reverse time and trace a particular mental experience back through progressively earlier stages in its development we would encounter softer and softer levels of mental activity. Eventually, when we arrived at the point in time when the thought was only on the point of being generated, we would reach a state of zero mental activity, a state of non-vibrating consciousness.

This state of mental stillness can be thought of in terms of pure consciousness or the true Self (see Chapter 8). In terms of the bubble analogy it is the bed of the pond from which the thought bubbles begin their journey upwards. Maharishi talks of it as the source of thought and a field of pure creative intelligence.

Every mental activity is, by virtue of its being an activity, a change of some kind. Maharishi sees change as a manifestation of the creative principle in nature. For him 'creativity' signifies not just inspired or original change but any change.

All thoughts also have a meaning of some kind; they are concerned with some thing. This directedness of thinking Maharishi sees as the expression of 'intelligence' – 'that which gives order and direction to change'.

He sees creativity and intelligence (in his sense of the words) in every thought and at every level of thought. Therefore, he argues, the source of thought from which all thoughts arise must be a field of pure creativity and pure intelligence – pure creative intelligence.

Many people might find this a bewildering concept. For the present we could interpret Maharishi as saying that the source of thought is a field of potential change and potential order. Most people learn the TM technique quite happily without fully grasping this point and for the present it will not affect our understanding of the TM process. We shall, however, return to it later (pp. 93 and 151).

The Source and the Causes of Thought

It is important that we should make ourselves clear of the distinction between the 'source of a thought' and the 'cause of a thought'. By the *source* of thought Maharishi denotes the field from which all thinking springs, every thought we ever have starts from deep within the mind as the faintest mental impulse and grows until it reaches consciousness. This is true of all thoughts whatever their meaning. It is the fundamental mechanism of all mental activity and is happening continuously from birth to death. What *causes* a thought to have a particular meaning is, however, a different process. We all know how one thought can spark off another and how some outside event will set us thinking about something else. When we ask what causes a certain thought we usually mean what previous ideas or incidents have given rise to this particular idea? We could say that the source relates to the medium in which mental activity is structured, whereas the cause determines the specific form this structure takes on.

This distinction can be made clearer by considering the analogous process which happens with a television picture. The picture is generated by a beam of electrons streaming from the cathode at the back of the tube. These are shaped and ordered by electrical and magnetic fields so that by the time the beam reaches the screen it produces a meaningful pattern of dots. The *source* of the picture is the cathode sitting at the back of the tube. What *causes* the initially unstructured stream of electrons to take on the form of one particular image is a chain of events which can be traced back through the electronics of the set, the aerial and the transmitter to the studio, and back further to producers, script writers, audience demands, political pressures, financial limitations, etc. In a similar way infinitely complex chains of events taking place in the world and in our brains *cause* the stream of thought impulses to take on a specific structure and meaning. But the *source* from which they spring is always the same.

The TM Process

The TM process is one of allowing the stronger levels of mental activity to reduce permitting the subtler underlying levels to enter consciousness. Maharishi defines the technique as 'turning the attention inwards towards the subtler levels of a thought until the mind transcends the subtlest state of the thought and arrives at the source of thought'.[3]

As the whole of mental activity settles down the threshold for conscious experience (the dotted line in Figure 2) is lowered and thoughts begin to enter the conscious mind at earlier stages in their development.

It is rather like being in a group of people at a cocktail party. In order to make yourself heard against all the background activity you have to raise your voice. This corresponds to the normal levels of thinking where thoughts have to become 'loud' enough to be experienced. If everybody in the room began to talk very softly you would no longer need to shout in order to be heard. Similarly during the TM technique all other mental 'chatter' has died away and the mind only needs to whisper an idea for it to be consciously appreciated. Finally, when the whole mind becomes perfectly still, thinking as we normally know it ceases and one is left in a state of 'pure consciousness' – the still source of thought.

This state is not only peaceful, it is also profoundly satisfying. And it is because the goal of meditation is itself an enjoyable state that it is not necessary to control the mind during meditation. Once one has begun to experience the satisfaction of the goal the attention will spontaneously settle down of its own accord without any individual coercion or effort.

Why, one might ask, does this not happen anyway, without a technique of meditation?

From early childhood onwards we have been encouraged to seek satisfaction in the world of sensory experience. Western society encourages this outer-directedness further by providing endless sources of entertainment, continually re-affirming that satisfaction can be gained through sensory experience of one form or another. So we keep looking for a source of stable satisfaction in the outer world – a world where all satisfactions are transitory – because this is the only way we know how to look.

Idries Shah, the Sufi teacher, makes this point in one of his Nasrudin stories.[4] A man saw Nasrudin searching for something on the ground. 'What have you lost, Mulla?' he asked.

'My key,' said the Mulla.

So the man went down on his knees too, and they both looked for it.

After a time, the other man asked: 'Where exactly did you drop it?'

'In my own house.'

'Then why are you looking here?'

'There is more light here than inside my own house.'

Similarly we have lost the inner 'key' to true fulfilment. It is lost within ourselves but we search for it outwardly because that is the only way we know how to look.

The reason why this inner source of satisfaction remains hidden is that it is over-shadowed by the grosser levels of mental activity. Indeed, the more we bombard the senses in our search for satisfaction the more mental noise increases, the stronger thoughts have to become in order to be consciously appreciated, and the more the inner fields are hidden from the awareness.

But although the source of thought itself remains hidden from the awareness the qualities associated with this field do nevertheless radiate out to some extent. In much the same way a light will shine out through a fog although the lamp itself may remain invisible, and the closer that one approaches the source the brighter the light becomes. Similarly, the subtler levels of thought are found to be of a more charming nature and once turned in the right direction the attention is drawn in spontaneously. As layer after layer is progressively peeled away the brilliance of the source increases and the attention is led on by the increasing charm to be found at every step, till finally it passes beyond even the finest level of thinking and arrives at a state of inner silence. The whole process is self-reinforcing; no control or effort is needed, it simply happens of its own accord.

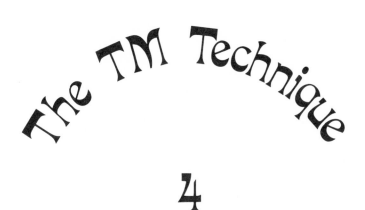

The TM Technique

4

'I think I'll go and meet her,' said Alice, for, though the flowers were very interesting, she felt that it would be far grander to have a talk with a real Queen.

'You can't possibly do that,' said the Rose: 'I should advise you to walk the other way.'

This sounded nonsense to Alice so she said nothing, but set off at once towards the Red Queen. To her surprise, she lost sight of her in a moment, and found herself walking in at the front-door again.

A little provoked, she drew back and, after looking everywhere for the Queen (whom she spied out at last, a long way off), she thought she would try the plan, this time, of walking in the opposite direction.

It succeeded beautifully. She had not been walking a minute before she found herself face to face with the Red Queen, and full in sight of the hill she had been so long aiming at.

Alice Through the Looking Glass

One of the commonest mistakes made in meditation is to *try* to reach the state of pure consciousness. But it turns out that trying only takes one further from the goal and like Alice one keeps returning to the starting point. It is only when one stops *trying* to meditate that the whole process starts happening of its own accord bringing one full in sight of the goal so long aimed at.

The idea that the mind has to be controlled before it will come to a state of stillness is usually the result of an incorrect understanding of how the mind functions. Many have noticed how their minds always seem to be wandering from one thought to another; never being still for long on one idea, let alone completely silent; a continually changing panorama of thoughts and images. They have assumed that it must therefore be in the nature of the mind to wander. From this false premise it is then deduced that if the mind is to be stilled it must be controlled: it must be prohibited from following its natural inclination.

Indian writings have summed this up by likening the mind to a monkey continually jumping from branch to branch. Monkeys, it is said, are naturally mischievous creatures and the only way in which you will keep a monkey still is to tie it down. The same, it is said, is true of the mind. The only way in which the continually wandering mind can be 'tamed' is to tie it down. And, since the mind loves to wander, this will be very difficult and require great effort.

As a result a vast range of practices have developed with the expressed intention of 'controlling the mind'. Some of these aim at holding the attention to one thought while others try to keep the mind empty of all thoughts. Whatever the technique it is invariably taught that effort and discipline will be essential if any success is to be gained.

But unless the thought or image to which the mind is being held is a particularly charming one the mind will soon become bored and start wandering off in search of more enjoyable experiences. It becomes 'obvious' that severe mental discipline will be essential if the mind is to be kept on the chosen theme. So one tries hard, and, lo and behold, it is indeed found to be difficult. Experience supports the argument and the fundamental flaw is never suspected. It is the initial premise that is wrong – the premise that it is the essential nature of the mind to wander.

A wise monkey-catcher realizes that the monkey is leaping from branch to branch for a reason; it is looking for something – more bananas perhaps. He realizes that to chase the monkey round and round the tree is a waste of time. It is much simpler and much quicker to place a pile of bananas at the foot of the tree and the monkey will soon come down of its own accord. By recognizing the inner needs of the monkey he brings it to a state of stillness without any effort, control or chaining down.

Similarly with the wandering mind. The essential nature of the mind is not to wander but to move towards sources of greater satisfaction. When the world changes or when we become bored the attention shifts elsewhere looking for more satisfaction. It is only because nothing in the external world offers a lasting satisfaction that the mind is continually wandering. Thus it is much simpler and quicker to open the awareness to the source of satisfaction lying within and then allow the mind to settle down of its own accord without any effort or control.

The Path of Effortlessness

Looking back over history we find that time and again the original teachings affirmed that meditation should be easy and gentle. But the passage of time has caused the original practices to become distorted and lose their effectiveness. Any claims that meditation was simple were quickly scoffed at and people began to interpret the original teachings in terms of control and effort.

Reading through the ancient texts one may often come across statements such as 'the mind must become still', or words to that effect. Now such a statement is very neutral. It merely states what must come to pass if any progress is to be made. It does not explicitly advocate effort or control in the process. But those who lacked the means to fulfil this recommendation saw this in the only way they could, in terms of control. They tended to translate it more in the sense that 'the mind must be made still'.

A controlled mind, however, is one of the fruits of meditation not a path to it. The very act of trying causes mental activity to increase and hinders meditation. Like *trying* to go to sleep at night: if you worry about going to sleep you only become more active and restless, but if you can completely forget about sleep – by counting sheep perhaps – then you will usually drop off without realizing it.

The purpose of meditation is to let the whole mind become completely still. But so long as there is any control or effort some mental activity must be continuing and it will be impossible for the *whole* mind to become still. Like trying to pull oneself up by one's own bootstraps – the more one tries the more one has to overcome. If one succeeds at all through effort then it is more than likely that one only succeeds in *thinking* that the mind has become still. (This does not necessarily mean that such practices can never work. They may eventually bear fruit, but only after a long and arduous ordeal – indeed, their proponents have never claimed otherwise. One possible explanation of how these techniques may eventually succeed is that after the mind has been stretched to its furthest limits for long periods of time it eventually gives up. When it does give up it lets go of *everything* and the person spontaneously 'transcends'.)

Likewise, concentration plays no part in the TM technique. Strictly speaking 'to concentrate' means to focus, to bring together, to become one-pointed; it does not necessarily signify control or effort. In most practical situations, however, some effort is usually necessary. Firstly the mind has to be held to the chosen thought against its natural tendency to roam off in search of more charming ideas. And secondly more energy has to be put into the thinking process itself in order to increase the signal-to-noise ratio and make the chosen thought clearer in consciousness. Thus the word 'concentration' has generally become synonymous with 'effort'.

In the TM technique the mind becomes concentrated of its own accord without any effort. The state of complete mental stillness is itself charming to the attention. One is now flowing *with* the natural tendency of the mind rather than struggling *against* it and control is no longer necessary. Moreover, since the background mental noise is decreasing, there is no need to think 'harder' in order to increase the clarity of thought – it becomes clearer automatically.

Another common error has been to mistake the source of thought for the cause of a thought. Various techniques have developed in which the person attempts to follow a thought back through its causal chain and through memory to its origin at some distant point in the past. But this is not the same as tracing a thought back to its source, i.e. experiencing the *same* thought at quieter and quieter levels of activity. Such practices are still concerned with the meaning of thoughts and hold the attention to the grosser levels of mental activity. They may be of some psychoanalytic value, but they are unlikely to lead the mind to a state of stillness.

With the TM technique there is no concern with the meaning of thoughts. It does not matter what one is thinking about, only that one can think. A point which Maharishi sums up by: 'Anyone who can think can meditate.' One's ideas may be useful, boring, clear, dull, brilliant or nonsensical but as far as the TM technique is concerned they are all thoughts of one form or another, and all thoughts, no matter what they are about or who is thinking them, start from the faintest impulse and develop until they are strong enough to be consciously appreciated. It is this structure of the thinking process which is the concern of the TM technique.

Some people have had the good fortune to arrive spontaneously at states of deep meditation, often without any prior knowledge of their existence let alone any deliberate attempt to reach them. In such cases one usually finds that the experience came when the person was relaxed and doing nothing in particular, letting the mind just wander according to its own nature. Here is part of R. M. Bucke's description of the mood which preceded his experience of the state. Note the relaxed, non-disciplined attitude of mind:[1]

> My mind . . . was calm and peaceful. I was sitting in a state
> of quiet, even passive enjoyment, not actually thinking, but
> letting ideas, images, and emotions flow of themselves. . . .

It is this passive attitude of letting things flow by themselves which is so important: not control or effort. The principal reason why these experiences do not happen more frequently is that we are always making an effort to succeed. In most spheres of life it may be true that the harder we try at something the more likely we are to achieve the goal, but it is simply not true of the TM technique. Here the less effort the better. Thus our attitude of continually trying and focusing the mind effectively removes the possibility of this natural occurrence from our lives.

The TM technique, by letting the mind slip into a state of silence of its own accord, is a means of allowing this natural state to occur more frequently and regularly and makes the experience available to everyone rather than just the fortunate or 'chosen' few.

Turning the Attention Within

The TM process might be summarily described as turning the attention through 180°: away from the outer world of sensory experience towards the subtler inner levels of the mind.

But this does not entail thinking about inner experiences, or about pure consciousness, for thinking *about something* inevitably keeps the attention on the level of meaning, i.e. on the surface levels of the mind. It does not have the effect of turning the attention within in the sense in which I use it here – the direct *experience* of the quieter underlying levels of thinking. As far as the TM technique is concerned, thinking about meditation is as much an outward directed activity as driving a car is. The inward turn that is necessary is a turning of the attention away from the meaning of thoughts and from all sensory experience.

When people first hear of the TM technique they quite naturally try to conceive of the process in terms of experiences with which they are already familiar. That is they form a mental image of the state. If then, without any further guidance they were to attempt to meditate they would almost certainly expect something similar to their image of the technique to be happening. But this would keep the attention on the senses and would still be a mental activity of some kind: it could not therefore be a true state of inner silence. This was emphasized six hundred years ago by the anonymous author of *The Cloud of Unknowing*, one of the first English works on contemplative mysticism:[2]

> They read and hear it said that they should stop the 'exterior' working with their mind, and work interiorly. And because they do not know what this 'interior' work means, they do it wrong. For they turn their actual physical minds inwards towards their bodies, which is an unnatural thing, and they strain as if to see spiritually with their physical eyes, and to hear within with their outward ears, and to smell and taste and feel and so on inwardly in the same way. So they pervert the natural order, and with this false ingenuity they put their minds to such unnecessary strains that ultimately their brains are turned. And at once the devil is able to deceive them with false lights and sounds, sweet odours and wonderful tastes, glowing and burning in their hearts or stomachs, backs or loins or limbs.

Any preconceptions or expectations of what will happen cannot help the process one iota. They can only hinder it. Moreover, any intellectual analysis or scrutiny of what is taking place will pull the mind back towards meaning and the surface levels of thought.

Thus Maharishi, in common with many teachers in the past, refrains from giving detailed descriptions of the meditative experience lest the pupil, in his eagerness to reach the goal, should turn himself away from the correct path.

Maharishi also emphasizes that one should not make any attempt to forget about the surface levels of thought:[3]

> Trying to forget amounts to remembering what one aims to forget. This should not be done because the process of meditation does not advance on the basis of forgetting the gross material objective world of possessions, but on the basis of entertaining finer fields of experience. The attempt to forget is based on hatred and condemnation, whereas the spontaneous experience of finer fields of thought during the meditation is based on that willing acceptance which is the natural tendency of the mind on the way to greater happiness. . . .

But equally one should not *try* not to anticipate, not to analyse, or not to forget. Trying of any kind increases mental activity and just as fatally holds the attention to the surface levels of thought.

Nor, therefore, should you *try* not to try!

It is impossible to coerce the mind inwards, it must be allowed to retire effortlessly and gradually of its own accord. Nothing can be done to hasten the process: 'Once begun, it should be allowed to proceed by itself . . . quietly and patiently, without any anxiety or hurry . . . naturally and innocently.'

The Technique of No-Technique

The basic principle of the TM technique is simply that of taking the correct initial attitude, the *effect* of which is that the attention begins to experience a thought at slightly earlier stages in its development. The whole system settles down a little and the attention, attracted by the charm of a slightly quieter level of thinking steps down again. And so it continues. The process entails nothing more than setting the correct initial conditions – the effortless inward turn of the attention – and letting go. The rest follows as surely and naturally as an apple falls to the ground.

Maharishi brings out a parallel here with the principle of least action in physics. The quantity 'action' is a measure of the energy exchange in any physical interaction and is the product of energy and time (or momentum and distance moved). The principle of least action states that for any given change in the physical world the total action involved will be the minimum possible within the limits imposed by the physical constraints of the given situation. This principle determines the path and velocity of a ball rolling down a slope. It determines the shape of the field around a magnet and the path of light rays as they are bent by different mediums. In fact given the initial conditions of any physical system and the constraints applying to it one may predict all future states of the system on the one assumption that any changes will satisfy the principle of least action. The principle is fundamental to the whole of classical mechanics.

Maharishi, however, sees it as being even more fundamental. It is not, he claims, restricted to the physical world, but can be applied to mental processes as well. We cannot test this statement in any quantitative way since at present we have no way of measuring 'mental energy'. Here I shall be concerned only with the qualitative implications of this hypothesis. Applying it specifically to the TM process he states that having set the correct initial conditions the mind will not only settle down to quieter levels of thinking automatically but will do so in the most efficient manner possible. Once set on the correct path there is nothing that we can do to hasten the process. It is as predetermined and as effortless as the arc of a diver.

Moreover you do not have to believe in the TM technique for it to work. Providing that you do make the correct start and do let go you will be carried down by the mind's search for satisfaction – by mental gravity one could say – whether you believe in it or not, just as the diver is carried down by physical gravity whether he believes it or not.

It may seem paradoxical, but the less you believe in it, the better. Those who come to the TM program with the expectation that here is something fantastic which will produce amazing experiences and immediate changes in their lives are apt to anticipate and analyse in their practice. They lose the innocence of approach that is so essential and which is retained by the person who starts by expecting little or is even highly skeptical.

The TM technique is not so much a 'doing' as a 'not-doing'. As such it is very reminiscent of the oriental concepts of the 'wayless-way' and the 'pathless-path'. Maharishi is very much in sympathy with teachers both East and West who have denounced techniques which involve 'doing' of any kind. But this does not mean that one should not do anything. There is a subtle but very important distinction between effortless meditation and doing nothing-in-particular.

People are sometimes suspicious of the TM technique precisely because it is called a technique. Enlightenment they say lies in knowledge of oneself and not in techniques. In part this is true: enlightenment does lie in knowledge of oneself, but this does not mean that one must also discover the path to enlightenment for oneself. That would imply that we should not learn from the experience of others. If we had seriously followed this principle in the past then most of us would still be sitting in caves wondering how to make a fire. What Maharishi is trying to do is to show other people how they too can reach a state of profound mental and physical silence.

The beauty of the TM technique is that it allows a person to come to a state of complete stillness and inactivity through using an activity – but an activity which spontaneously reduces all activity including itself. It is this ability of the TM technique to transcend itself as a technique which makes it so effective. In fact any technique which did not finally transcend itself along with all other mental activity could never take the mind to a state of complete silence.

Mantras

During the TM technique one experiences a given thought at progressively earlier stages in its development. But not just any thought would be suitable for this: it has to have specific qualities which allow the attention to step down from the normal gross levels of thinking and appreciate the finer underlying levels.

The first requirement is that it should be a thought without meaning. Any thought which has a meaning – and virtually every thought does – will hold the attention to the surface levels of thinking. So a thought is chosen which has no meaningful associations. This thought could be derived from any of the senses. It could, for instance, be a meaningless visual image. But it is generally held that the sense of hearing is the most suitable. This may be because we are used to thinking verbally. It may also have relevance to the fact that hearing is the last sense to disappear during the onset of an anaesthetic.

Now not any meaningless sound would do. It is obviously going to be more conducive to meditation if the sound is soothing rather than jarring or agitating. To take an example of the latter, the sound of finger nails scraping down glass may not contain much meaning but for most people it would not have a very soothing quality and would not be a very suitable sound for meditation! The sounds used in the TM technique are ones which resonate with the nervous system in a soothing harmonious manner.

Until recently many would have scoffed at the idea that the choice of sound was so important. But Western science is now beginning to discover that sounds do indeed have profound effects on living organisms. It has, for example, been found that some bacteria will thrive when certain notes are played and die when subjected to others, and plants will grow better when played the Brandenberg Concertos than when subjected to heavy rock music.[4] And it has been discovered that certain algae display genetic-like mutations after being subjected to the sound of a sledge hammer – and that only that particular sledge hammer vibration would have the effect.[5] Roberto Assagioli, an Italian psychologist of whom I shall have more to say later, bases much of his work on the belief that music can both cause disease and cure it.[6] And the work of Hans Jenny and others has shown how specific vibratory patterns in time can produce intricate three-dimensional patterns in space which are often very reminiscent of simple life forms.[7] So the suggestion that specific sounds can have particular effects on the individual does not appear to be so far-fetched.

The sounds which are used in the TM technique are called *mantras* and are taken from the ancient Vedic tradition of India which has always recognized the intimate relationship between sound and form. The long-term effects of these sounds are just as important as their effects within meditation, and mantras are traditionally divided into two categories, recluse mantras and 'householder' mantras.

The recluse mantras have the general effect of supporting a withdrawn, recluse way of life. The householder mantras on the other hand support the way of life of a person engaged in worldly affairs.

Unfortunately this distinction has often become very muddled and recluse mantras have been given to active 'householders'. When the original teachings became distorted and lost it was always the householder practices which were lost first: the recluse practices were not so widely disseminated and remained in a purer form. Thus when at some later date a person wished to take up meditation he naturally turned to the monks and hermits for instruction, they being the only ones to have preserved some remnants of the original. But they invariably gave out their own reclusive practices with the result that the meditation led to a withdrawal from activity. This seemingly confirmed the idea that a recluse life was the only path to enlightenment.

Just how important it is to have the correct type of mantra is revealed by those cases in which people have decided to teach themselves the TM technique. Some 'friend' may have described the technique – even though the technique is not easily described – and the enthusiastic aspirants then chose some mantra for themselves, usually from some book or other. They then began the 'TM' technique – or so they thought. Within a short time, however, they were puzzled to find the qualities of their lives slowly deteriorating and the desire to engage in normal activities decreasing. This was not at all what they expected of the TM technique. Faced with this disappointment some gave up the whole idea of meditation, while others sought correct instruction and began to gain better results.

A few people have published their mantras in books and magazine articles, usually with the intention of saving other people the trouble of going along to a TM center in order to learn the TM technique. But the mantra itself, although necessary, is only part of the technique: it is far more important to be shown the correct method of using the mantra, for without this there is very little chance of any success. This is one reason why TM instructors give out the mantras only during actual TM instruction.

Another, and in many respects more important, reason why the mantras are kept quiet is because saying one's mantra aloud can disturb the technique itself. During the TM technique the mantra is being experienced at quieter, more abstract levels of mental activity, and after a while becomes associated more with these subtler levels of thinking. To say the mantra aloud is giving it a concrete expression. This is the opposite direction to the TM process and is likely to interfere with the practice, making it less effective.

For similar reasons one should not make a subvocal repetition of the mantra. This is a very important distinction between the TM technique and other practices involving mantras. Nearly all other practices which make use of mantras involve a constant repetition of the sound, either out loud as a verbal chant or as a subvocal repetition. In India this procedure is often called *mantra-japa* ('Japa' meaning a 'constant repetition') and the intention is to keep up a continuous repetition of the sound, often with the aim of filling the mind with the *idea* of the devotional object, usually some deity, in the hope of gaining some spiritual union.

It is possible that many of these practices arose from misunderstandings and distortions of TM-like practices. If, for example, we look back to the teachings of Shankara, one of the principal sources of contemporary Indian practices, we find him clearly contradicting repetitious practices when he declares that 'deliverance is not achieved by repeating the words "Brahman", but by directly experiencing Brahman. . . .'[8] Sadly Shankara's teachings have now been turned upside down and most of his modern 'followers' indulge in the unending repetition of 'Brahman' or some similar word.

All such practices bind the attention to the gross surface levels of the mind and do not allow experience of the subtler levels of thought nor of the field of pure consciousness beyond all thought. In the TM technique the mantra has no associations and, more importantly, is not chanted – either verbally or mentally. The mantra is not so much an object for the attention to be focused on as a vehicle on which the attention rests and which leads it down to the subtler levels of thinking. This is brought about by the passive rather than active nature of the technique, the meaninglessness of the chosen sound, and the greater charm of the finer levels which allow the attention to be spontaneously drawn within.

Personal Guidance

Unfortunately the actual TM technique cannot be written down; it can only be taught through practice and with personal guidance. I say 'unfortunately' for Maharishi's professed aim is to spread the TM technique as fast as possible, and he would be the first to seize upon any chance of speeding its propagation. But it is also Maharishi's aim to spread the *TM* technique; to ensure that it is the TM technique which is taught and not something else.

He explains fully this need for personal guidance in *The Science of Being*:[9]

The practice of transcendental meditation has to be imparted by personal instruction. It cannot be imparted through a book, because the teacher must not only show the aspirant how to experience the subtle states of thinking but should also be responsible for checking his experiences as he proceeds on that path.

Experiences vary from man to man. Therefore it is not practical to record all the possible experiences. Nor is it to the advantage of the beginner to know in advance all that it is possible for him to experience.

... The moment one begins to experience the subtle states of thought, one finds oneself drifting towards increasingly abstract states of experience. It takes a while for the beginner to be able to pinpoint his experience of subtle states of thought, even with the help of a personal teacher. For this reason it is of no practical value to describe in writing the details of the practice. The practice of transcendental meditation must always be taught by expert masters of meditation, who have been trained to impart it accurately as well as to check experience.

TM Research

5

There is a difficulty which bedevils nearly all attempts to measure subjects during the TM technique. The very act of measuring people disturbs them both physiologically and psychologically, making the meditation shallower than normal.

I have known of researchers asking subjects to practise the technique while laden down with tubes and wires, with recording devices clicking and buzzing away close by, and with technicians scurrying around. It is hardly surprising that under these conditions only slight changes are recorded. This does not discredit the TM technique: it only shows that under such intrusive conditions the TM technique yields less significant data.

It is fairly easy to eliminate these physical sources of disturbance by making the apparatus and experimenters less obtrusive, but there is still the far more persistent problem of psychological disturbance. Just the knowledge that one is being measured can upset the TM process. This can happen in two ways.

Firstly, the TM technique is an entirely innocent and effortless process. Meditators remain absorbed in the enjoyable nature of their experience and usually do not even notice that the body and mind are both becoming very still. But in an experimental situation they inevitably become a little more aware of the changes taking place in themselves. This slight shift of attitude, small as it may be, will interfere with the practice to some extent. Subjects from several TM experiments have reported that meditation was not as deep as normal during experimentation.

Breathing may be one of the easiest physiological parameters to measure during meditation but it is also the most easily disturbed. One of the first doctors to conduct research on the TM technique reported that it took more than two months of daily meditation in the experimental situation to accustom the subject to the apparatus. Only then did he begin to record the very slow, shallow patterns of breathing characteristic of the Transcendental Meditation technique.

The second difficulty is that subjects would, quite understandably, like to produce good results. I am not suggesting that they start consciously trying to produce good results – any meditator knows how futile and disastrous that would be – but deep inside there arises a slight eagerness for a 'good' meditation. With this faintest degree of anticipation they lose the all-important innocence of approach and the practice immediately loses its effectiveness.

Gradually these difficulties are being overcome, and experiments are now revealing some very interesting physiological changes which suggest that the body may well be passing into a unique state during the TM technique.

Metabolic Activity

The overall rate at which the body consumes energy is measured by the *metabolic rate*. The more active we are the more energy we use and the higher, therefore, the metabolic rate. It is usually assumed that there is a lower limit to metabolic activity, called the basal metabolic rate, which can be thought of as the minimum energy necessary to keep the body 'ticking over' when sitting or lying still. In deep sleep the rate can fall to about 10 per cent below the basal level but much below this has generally been considered very unusual and even abnormal for human beings.

Since oxygen is one of our prime sources of energy the metabolic rate is reflected in the rate and depth of our breathing. So, when early TM meditators noticed their breathing becoming very slow and shallow they naturally assumed a considerable reduction in their metabolic rate.

The first objective analysis of these changes was carried out in 1965 in London. Dr John Allison measured the rate of breathing and found that it changed from the customary dozen or so breaths per minute of normal rest to an average of six breaths per minute during the TM technique.[1] This is very low, though not abnormally so – one could achieve this without meditating by taking very deep breaths; what was particularly striking was that the six or so breaths per minute during the TM technique were so shallow as to be hardly detectable. This meant that the subject was not compensating for his slowed breathing by taking in more air each breath; on the contrary he was taking in far less air each breath. A respiratory physiologist estimated that such a breathing pattern was consistent with a drop in metabolic rate of around 75 per cent below the basal level. He commented that anyone who did that for twenty minutes should, by all accounts, be dead: but the subject was very much alive!

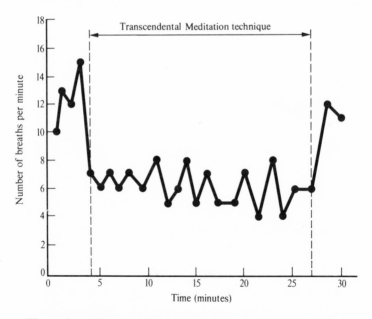

Figure 3   *Change in breath rate during the TM technique.*
© Lancet. *Reproduced by kind permission of* Lancet *and the author.*

The implication that oxygen consumption was decreasing was confirmed in 1970 by Dr Keith Wallace in America. Wallace measured the oxygen consumption directly and found that during the TM technique there was an average fall in consumption of 16 per cent below the basal level.[2] The reason that his subjects did not show as slow or shallow a breathing as Allison's was probably because the apparatus was more disturbing and little time was allowed for the subjects to get used to the experimental situation.

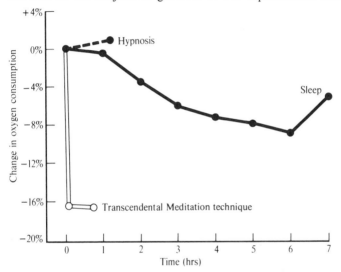

Figure 4   *Change in oxygen consumption. From 'The Physiology of Meditation' by R. K. Wallace and H. Benson. © 1972 by* Scientific American, Inc. *All rights reserved.*

Wallace also studied several other physiological variables. He found that the production of carbon dioxide – which results from the combustion of oxygen – decreased by the same amount as oxygen consumption. Thus less oxygen was being used up by the body and this suggests that the reduced breathing was the consequence of a reduced need for oxygen. This hypothesis is supported by two other observations. First, there was no compensatory over-breathing after practising the TM technique, i.e. the body did not have to make up for any lack of oxygen. And second, measurements of the gases dissolved in the blood showed normal levels of oxygen and carbon dioxide.

When we are very active the carbon dioxide level increases and the body compensates for this by increasing the rate and depth of breathing. Conversely, when the carbon dioxide level falls below the optimum breathing slows down. Wallace's findings show the optimum levels of both gases being maintained throughout the TM technique. The reduced rate and depth of breathing must therefore be a *result* of reduced metabolic activity. If it were the *cause* there would be a deficit of oxygen in the blood and a build-up of carbon dioxide.

Unfortunately this distinction has often been missed and many have supposed that a state of inner tranquillity could be achieved by imitating the reduced breathing patterns of those they had observed in a state of calm and mental peace. But deliberately restricting the breathing will only cause oxygen starvation and a mild carbon dioxide poisoning of the brain. This may well produce an altered state of consciousness but it is certainly not the same state as that reached with the TM program.

It is important to realize that neither the body nor the brain are deprived of oxygen during the TM technique. The oxygen available in the blood remains at its normal level; it is simply that the body's requirements have been reduced. Mothers-to-be sometimes fear that such reduced levels of oxygen consumption might be dangerous for the unborn child. But as far as the foetus is concerned the amount of oxygen available in the blood has not changed and it is no more deprived of oxygen than the mother is.

People practising the TM technique have often reported that during the deepest states of meditation their breathing dies away completely. This is quite a remarkable claim, but one that nevertheless now appears to be valid. In Switzerland a special laboratory has been established, employing the most modern apparatus and computing techniques, to examine the TM state in depth. Experiments there on advanced TM subjects have found that during those periods when the mind is completely silent and devoid of normal thought activity the breathing does indeed disappear.

Subjects were asked to press a button whenever they had experienced a period of transcendental consciousness – the name given to the state of complete mental silence. Since all thoughts have ceased during the state it would obviously be impossible for a subject to signal to the experimenter while he was in the state, but by getting him to signal immediately afterwards it was possible to look back and examine what changes had been taking place in the preceding period.

It was found that on every occasion that the subject indicated a period of transcendental consciousness the breathing had come to a complete standstill. These periods lasted for between 10 and 35 seconds. As before there was no compensatory over-breathing afterwards – indeed the breathing when it returned was still much slower than normal – and there was no build up of carbon dioxide in the blood. Measurements of the amount of oxygen consumed showed a reduction in metabolic rate of 40 to 60 per cent.[3]

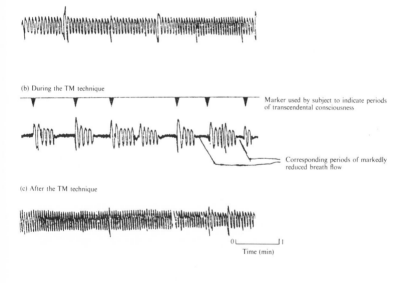

(a) Before the TM technique

(b) During the TM technique

Marker used by subject to indicate periods of transcendental consciousness

Corresponding periods of markedly reduced breath flow

(c) After the TM technique

Time (min)

Figure 5   *Breathing patterns before, during and after the Transcendental Meditation technique, showing periods of markedly reduced breathing during the technique. © Maharishi European Research University, 1976.*

Measurements of other variables such as skin resistance and brain activity showed that this state was clearly distinguishable from waking, dreaming and deep sleep, and it has been postulated to represent a fourth major state of consciousness (see Chapter 8).

Such results it should be emphasized are generally found in people with more experience of the TM technique. In a study of 95 subjects, 10 showed periods when the breathing died away completely. These ten had been practising the TM technique for between three and eight years, and eight of them were participating in a special residential program.[4] Thus it is not surprising to find that in experiments using comparatively naïve subjects such results may not be easily reproducible.

There is a wide variation in the effects measured during the TM technique. In one study in Seattle it was found that four out of five subjects were showing changes very similar to sleep and it was suggested that sleeping could account for the beneficial effects of the TM program.[5] However, just because in this case some sleeping was observed does not mean that this is all there is to the technique. It is a common experience of most people who have learnt the TM technique that if they have had a particularly tiring day then they may find themselves taking short naps during their meditation – this is probably what was happening during the Seattle study. But it is also a common experience that there are many periods when the body and mind are in a very quiet state; one is fully conscious and definitely not asleep. It is after such periods that one feels the most fully rejuvenated.

The states of zero breathing and markedly reduced metabolism do, it is true, go far beyond the expectations of Western physiology, but we should not therefore discount them; a healthy skepticism should be balanced by an equally healthy open-mindedness. Furthermore, because the claims made for the TM program go beyond our present Western understanding of what is possible, beyond the current physiological paradigm, experiments in this field will need to be more convincingly designed and more strictly controlled than experiments investigating more orthodox phenomena if they are to pass the skeptical scrutiny of the scientific establishment.

Other Physiological Changes

Reduced breathing and oxygen consumption are the most obvious changes to take place during the TM technique but they are by no means the only changes. The results of several other research projects suggest that the TM technique affects nearly every aspect of the body's physiology.

Along with the reduction in breathing there is a decrease in heart rate of about 5 beats per minute[6] (ten beats per minute during transcendental consciousness[7]), and a decrease in cardiac output (the amount of blood pumped out by the heart) of about 25 per cent.[8] These changes show that the work load of the heart is being reduced. Blood pressure also decreases, especially in hypertensive people,[9] and this is related to the reduction in stress which the TM technique brings. These changes have been found to carry over into ordinary life showing that people are more relaxed during the day as a result.[10]

Analysis of the blood itself shows that a chemical called blood lactate, produced during strenuous physical activity and also associated with anxiety states, is eliminated from the system much more rapidly during the Transcendental Meditation technique.[11]

There are also changes in other biochemicals in the blood which indicate a general reduction in stress during and after the technique.[12]

Studies of brain activity with the EEG (electroencephalogram) show a relaxed but alert state of mental functioning. They have also revealed fascinating changes relating to the co-ordination of the two halves of the brain and I shall look at these in more detail shortly. Interesting changes in the electrical activity of the skin indicate a general decrease in anxiety and corresponding increase in stability and adaptability.[13] Many of these effects have been found to occur right from the very first TM session.

Besides these physiological experiments there are also studies which show a general improvement in health, decrease in insomnia, relief from asthma, decreased use of drugs (both prescribed and non-prescribed), faster reaction time, sharper perception, improved mind–body co-ordination, fuller development of personality, growth of creativity and intelligence, and improved interpersonal relationships. These studies and others will be discussed later in the book where they are more relevant.

Research into the TM program is expanding at such a rate that any information given in this book may well have been superseded by the time it reaches the reader. All the studies have been put together in a book of collected papers and I recommend anyone who wants further details of the research to refer to it and its future editions.[14]

Yoga and Zen

The yogic teachings of the East have always held that the deepest state of meditation, the state of *samadhi,* or 'stilled mind' is also a state of complete physical stillness; a state of suspended animation – but a conscious one.

Scientific investigations into the claims of yogis have suffered the same difficulties as the research into the TM program. Additionally they have been hampered by the vast variety of techniques employed, making any degree of uniformity difficult to achieve, and by the physical difficulty of getting delicate apparatus up to mountain retreats where many of the more adept practitioners live. Nevertheless the experiments that have been conducted generally reveal the same trend towards decreased metabolism as found in the TM technique. Similar changes have also been found in Zen monks in Japan.

It is significant that although the physiological effects of Yoga and Zen are in general similar to the TM program, it often takes many years, even a lifetime, of practice at these techniques to achieve states which are reached after only a year or two with the TM program. Maharishi never claims that the TM technique is the only way to a full inner development; he readily accepts that there are many practices which eventually lead to the same state. He does however maintain that the TM technique is the fastest way. In that most other practices teach some control or mental concentration they are, he claims, opposed to the mind's natural tendency to move towards greater satisfaction and are therefore not only arduous but circuitous routes to the goal.

A second difference is that most of the yogis and Zen masters studied in experiments tended to be recluses whereas the subjects in the TM experiments were all active people engaged in normal everyday lives. This supports Maharishi's claim that renunciation and retirement from the world are not prerequisites to meditation, and that the TM technique is particularly suitable to the 'householder'.

Biofeedback?

In recent years it has been demonstrated that it is possible to change many physiological variables previously thought to be beyond individual control. The subject 'learns' to control blood pressure, skin resistance or EEG activity not by deliberately trying to change them but by attending to information 'fed back' from monitoring instruments. The technique is known as 'biofeedback'. All the subject does is to try to find a mental state resulting in the correct physiological change. Since many of the changes which can be induced by such techniques are similar to those found in the TM technique it has been suggested that biofeedback might be a short cut to these states. Initially this suspicion was supported by the finding that the correct mental attitude for biofeedback was usually similar to that of meditation – 'a detached non-anxious, merely expectant' attitude.[15] But more recent work suggests that far from being a short cut to these states it may not even be a route at all.

Firstly, biofeedback falls down in that whilst most subjects find that they can produce one, or perhaps two, physiological changes by this method, it is not possible to produce a large number of changes in an integrated fashion as occurs with the TM technique. And secondly, with the TM technique no deliberate attempt is made to produce any physiological changes. They usually occur without the person being aware of them and come as the effects rather than the cause of a settling down of mental activity.

Self-hypnosis?

It is sometimes suggested that the TM technique might be nothing more than self-hypnosis. Leaving aside the rather cynical suggestion that through self-hypnosis a person can fool himself into believing almost anything, it is reasonable to note that self-hypnosis, involving the use of repetitious phrases or images, is often used as an aid to relaxation: could not the TM technique be based on similar principles and be having a similar effect?

The answer, I believe, is 'No'. On the first point the physiology of hypnosis is generally different from that of the TM technique. Even when a subject is given the hypnotic suggestion to relax completely it is found that despite muscular relaxation the metabolism does not change significantly, if anything it rises slightly (see Figure 4, p. 43). Furthermore, EEG recordings from the brain of a hypnotized subject usually show a waking pattern of activity (unless the subject is deliberately sent to sleep in which case he will show sleeping patterns) whereas with the TM technique the EEG patterns are different from both waking states and sleep states. These and other physiological differences argue against the TM technique being just some form of self-hypnosis.

Concerning the superficial similarity of the mantra to a hypnotic rhythm it should be remembered that the use of the mantra in the TM technique is not one of *continual* repetition. Such incessant repetition of sounds is known to have strange effects on perception but this does not satisfactorily explain the experience of the TM technique.

It is interesting that such theories about the mantra are generally put forward by non-meditators. One could argue that they had not therefore become biased towards Maharishi's explanation of the process. But I think it is more likely that they had not personally experienced, and therefore not fully understood, the important difference between continuous forms of repetition (such as in the Indian *mantra-japa* mentioned earlier) and the non-directed, passive awareness of the mantra which occurs in the TM technique. If it were just a matter of hypnotizing oneself with a repetitious phrase it would surely be more effective to make a steady subvocal repetition of the mantra in order that the nervous system habituate as easily and quickly as possible? But, as anyone who practises the TM technique will verify, such constant repetition does not readily lead to a state of restful alertness.

Mere Relaxation?

One obvious effect of the TM technique is to produce a profound state of mental and physical relaxation. But, as we shall see in Part Two, this is only part of the story, and it is important that the TM state should not be identified with a few physiological parameters. Ultimately it is the person's own state of consciousness which is important. Experiments are valuable in providing a degree of objective support for the claims of those practising the TM technique, and help us understand what is taking place in the body during the process. But they should not be taken to define the TM state, for that can only result in confusion.

Suppose, for example, that the only change we knew to occur during the TM technique was a reduction in heart rate of five beats per minute. If this became the definition of the TM state then anything that produced such a reduction could be said to be equivalent to the TM technique. Until, that is, further research showed other parameters which were changing. Unfortunately several researchers have already fallen into this trap. Dr Herbert Benson at Harvard, for example, claimed that by sitting and thinking the word 'One' on each outbreath it was possible to produce all the effects of the TM technique.[16] He originally showed that his technique could simulate the changes which he and Wallace had earlier found to be occurring during the TM technique (though work in Pennsylvania has now cast serious doubts on this claim[17]). Since Wallace's pioneering work on the TM program other studies have found that in deeper meditation the changes are more profound and that many other parameters are changing. These effects have not yet been observed in Dr Benson's relaxation technique. Indeed, from a theoretical point of view we should not expect his technique to lead on to deeper states of meditation. Apart from the fact that the word 'One' is not meaningless, it has a rougher quality than the TM mantras and would not be so conducive to a settling down of the mind. More importantly, his instruction to attach the word to the breathing is going to keep the attention channelled through the senses, and it is not easy to reach a state of transcendental consciousness whilst the mind is directed outwards rather than inwards.

EEG and Brain Synchrony

The electroencephalogram (EEG) detects the minute electrical changes occurring over the scalp as a result of activity within the brain. The patterns which are recorded can be analysed according to their component frequencies and the different frequencies can be correlated with different types of mental activity.

When, for example, the attention is sharply focused on some mental task there is a broad spectrum of activity ranging from 2 or 3 Hz to 30 or 40 Hz (Hz stands for Hertz, the frequency of a wave). This is called desynchronized activity. When the attention is not concentrated on anything in particular and the brain is, so to speak, free-wheeling most people show what is called alpha-activity. This consists of a predominance of waves in the 8 to 10 Hz waveband, particularly at the back of the head. When a person is in deep sleep his brain shows a predominance of very slow activity of the order of 1 and 2 Hz called delta-activity.

The EEG is still a very crude measurement of brain functioning. All that is being detected is the overall pattern of activity of millions of neurons. It is rather like hanging a microphone above a large city and recording the traffic noise. You might be able to tell whether it was rush hour or the middle of the night, or whether the traffic lights were changing in synchrony, but that is about all. Nevertheless, crude as it is, the EEG is the most convenient technique available for assessing the general activity of the brain and relating it to different states of consciousness.

During the TM technique there is found to be an abundance of alpha-activity indicating, not surprisingly, that the attention is unfocused and relaxed. This activity tends to be slower than normal (about 8 Hz rather than 9 or 10 Hz) and of larger amplitude.[18] It also spreads forward from the rear of the brain where it is usually found, to cover the whole of the scalp and at the same time appears to become synchronized in the sense that the waves from different areas of the scalp take the same form. In order to understand the significance of this synchronization it is necessary to know a little more about the functioning of the brain.

It has long been known that most nerves from the right side of the body end up on the left side of the brain and most from the left side of the body on the right side of the brain. So when you touch something with your right hand it is the left side of the brain which controls the movement and registers the sensation.

There are, however, many other ways in which the two halves of the brain differ in their functions. Various experiments over the last twenty years have shown that the major control of verbal, linguistic and rational functions appears to take place in the left hemisphere, while spatial relationships, image recognition, and aesthetic appreciation are largely controlled by the right hemisphere.[19]

Most of the functions associated with the left side of the brain involve a sequential or linear type of processing (i.e. one after the other) while most of the right side functions would appear to necessitate a simultaneous or parallel mode of processing. Speech and writing, for example, involve the analysis of an idea into a linear chain of words and phonemes which are then spoken or written one after the other, whereas the judgment of a spatial relationship requires the simultaneous appreciation of several factors and their synthesis into a whole.* Recent work in England has confirmed this hypothesis showing that the left side of the brain is better at functioning in a sequential manner while the right tends to operate more in a simultaneous manner.[20]

It used to be thought that the left hemisphere was the dominant or major hemisphere, but it now appears that neither side is fundamentally more dominant than the other. It is more a question of which functions we lay emphasis upon. It has been found that if a person is asked to perform some essentially linear task such as writing a letter, then the right side of the brain becomes relatively inactive, showing a higher proportion of alpha-activity, leaving the attention focused on the left. If, conversely, the subject is asked to draw a picture then the left passes into a state of comparative inactivity and the right concentrates on the problem. What is probably happening is that the half of the brain not directly concerned with the given task is being shut off in order to reduce the level of interference in the other half. In comparing the EEG patterns of different professional groups it has been found that people such as lawyers who concentrate upon analytic thinking show a left hemisphere dominance whereas artists show a right hemisphere dominance.

Our society lays greater emphasis on verbal and rational abilities with the result that the left has come to be regarded as the more important half. In school we were taught the three R's (reading, 'riting and 'rithmetic) – all left hemisphere functions – and those associated with the right were largely untouched. So it is not that the left is intrinsically more dominant, only that our emphasis on the left has caused it to become dominant in that most people use this mode for the major part of the day.

Robert Ornstein has suggested that one of the functions of meditative practices is to correct this by establishing a state of balance between the left and right hemispheres. In the case of the TM technique it certainly looks as if this may be the happening.

What is particularly interesting about the TM technique is the manner in which the alpha-activity builds up. Detailed analysis by Dr Bernard Glueck revealed that the alpha-activity built up first in the left hemisphere and then in the right,[21] suggesting that the

---

* Reading and writing do not have to be so linear. Techniques of speed reading seem to be using the right hemisphere as much, if not more, than the left. Most of us learnt to read by first vocalizing and then subvocalizing the words. This leaves the process firmly implanted in the left hemisphere. Speed readers seem to break this habit, and can take in several lines at once *visually* rather than one word at a time *verbally*. With writing there are techniques such as Tony Buzan's organic patterning of information which use non-linear, multi-dimensional forms of display, encouraging right hemisphere activity along with that of the left (Tony Buzan, *Use Both Sides of Your Brain*, Dutton, 1976).

active analytical mode was giving way to the receptive synthetic mode which was then itself being reduced. This relates very closely to the practice of the TM technique.

There are two fundamental aspects to the TM technique: the mantra and the technique of using it. Both together turn out to be conducive to a shift towards right hemisphere activity.

The mantra is meaningless and has no verbal associations. It does not therefore encourage the linguistic thinking normally associated with the left hemisphere. Furthermore in using the mantra one does not make any attempt at subvocal repetition, which would again be a left hemisphere activity.

The TM technique is very much a technique of not-doing, a passive awareness; one has the attitude of letting it happen rather than making it happen. There is no intellectual analysis of experiences. Consequently the rational analytic processes usually associated with the left hemisphere are not particularly encouraged. Thus the initial effect of the TM technique can be seen to be one of allowing the attention to shift more towards the right hemisphere.

But the TM technique is more than just a turn to right hemisphere activity – if it were only that it would be little different from sitting down and listening to some good music. The technique results in a transcending of both types of mental activity. It would appear that to start the process off one first has to reduce the more predominant, active mode of thought and *then* allow the other mode to decrease as well, until both come to a relaxed state. This is borne out by Glueck's work mentioned above and by Dr Jean-Paul Banquet, working at Harvard.

Banquet found that as a person passed deeper into the TM state there was a progressive 'synchronization' of the EEG patterns. He uses the word synchronization here in a slightly different way from which it is commonly used in EEG work. Usually one speaks of a synchronization of the activity of groups of cells, and it is this synchronization which gives rise to strong frequency components like the alpha-wave. Banquet extends the use of the word to cover the synchronization of activity from completely different areas of the brain – a much rarer phenomenon. In this type of synchrony not only are groups of cells displaying synchronous activity (i.e. alpha-activity) but all the alpha-activity of the cortex is of the same frequency and in phase.

He found that during the TM technique this synchronization

appeared first between the front and rear of the head and then between the left and right hemisphere. It was particularly striking in occasional bursts of faster brain activity (20 Hz) which usually occurred at moments when subjects felt themselves to be in a particularly deep state of meditation.[22]

Work at MERU (Maharishi European Research University) in Switzerland has thrown more light on this synchrony. Dr Paul Levine and his colleagues applied sophisticated techniques of computer analysis, originally developed for the processing of 'Over the Horizon Radar' signals, to the study of the coherence of EEG patterns. If two waveforms are of exactly the same frequency then their phase difference, that is the interval between corresponding peaks, will be constant over any given period. If, however, they are of slightly different frequencies their relative phase difference will be continually varying with time. The coherence is a measure of the stability of the phase difference; the lower the variability the greater the coherence. When the variability is zero the coherence is 100 per cent. In terms of brain activity it measures the correlation of activity between two different parts of the scalp.

Levine and his team found that during the TM technique there was usually strong coherence in the alpha band, beginning as soon as the person began the technique, and spreading to both the theta and beta bands. The coherence was detectable right from the very first day of learning the practice and was more pronounced the longer the subject had been using the technique. There was, however, little evidence of coherence during sleep or the ordinary waking state.[23] In advanced subjects it was found that the greatest coherence occurred during periods of transcendental consciousness, when the breathing had virtually disappeared.[24]

The plots in Figure 6 show coherence patterns over three thirty minute periods. Each horizontal line represents the coherence spectrum for a given five second interval. The humps on the line represent the degree of coherence at the respective frequency. Only coherence greater than 95 per cent is displayed (implying a frequency variation of less than 0.05 Hz). The lines are then drawn one behind the other to show the pattern of coherence over a full thirty minute session. The long ridges show coherence continuing over many minutes. In (b), for example, the coherence becomes noticeable as soon as the subject begins the technique and continues through into the eyes closed period at the end of the session.

Control Periods: EO – Eyes Open, EC – Eyes Closed (See text for description of display)

Figure 6   *Coherence patterns in: (a) sleep, (b) during the TM technique with subject of four months' experience, (c) during the TM technique with subject of fifteen years' experience.*
© *Maharishi European Research University, 1976.*

Because the right hemisphere is usually less active than the left its energy output is less. Mark Westcott, working in England, found that during the TM technique the relative energy outputs of the two halves were equalized. This state of balance continued after meditation as well. In fact the regular meditators started off the experiment with higher levels of balance indicating that the effects were lasting throughout the day. The controls who sat and merely 'relaxed' not only started off with lower levels of balance but the power ratio actually dropped during the experiment suggesting that they were using their left hemispheres in order to make themselves relax, rather than allowing it to happen.[25]

☐ Left hemisphere

▨ Right hemisphere

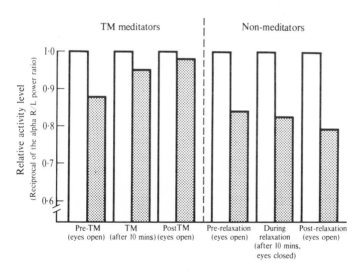

Figure 7   *Equalization of activity levels in left and right halves of brain during and after the TM technique.*

The implication of the EEG synchronization is that the person practising the TM technique does not have to suppress one side of his brain in order to attend to the messages coming from the other half, but can use both halves simultaneously. He or she can begin to live that long sought for synthesis of reason and intuition, art and science, and the union of Eastern and Western thought, a possibility which I shall return to in Chapter 13.

It may well be that Western science is now rediscovering something which has been known to the East for hundreds of years. Among the complex and diverse Tantric teachings of India and Tibet is a common claim that the breathing alternates between the left and right nostrils. Even when the nose is completely clear the breath will still flow predominantly through one of the nostrils. In the healthy person the breath is said to change from one nostril to the other every twenty minutes (some texts put the figure at exactly 24 minutes). The breath through the right nostril is called the sun breath. It is said that when breathing through this nostril the person should undertake actions involving physical exertion, combat, speech and discussion. The left nostril breath, called the moon breath, is said to be best for painting, composing, listening to music, etc. There is therefore a clear correlation between the left nostril and what we now believe to be right hemisphere activities and the right nostril and left hemisphere activities. This does not mean that when breathing through the left nostril the right hemisphere is dominant – this clearly is not the case: only that there is a predisposition for right hemisphere activity. The actual hemisphere in dominance still depends upon the specific activity being engaged in.

The most interesting claim made by the Tantric texts is that during transcendental consciousness the breath flows equally through both nostrils. This clearly parallels the recent finding that the two hemispheres are in balance during the deeper phases of meditation. Moreover it is written that the perfect individual maintains a state of balanced breath throughout the day. This we shall see later corresponds to the fully developed person who is able to maintain the inner stillness of meditation along with all activity, and represents a fifth state of consciousness.

The Relief of Stress

6

All men, especially the busy, secular as well as the religious should be taught meditation for it is a refuge to which one can retreat when faced with stressful situations.

from Francisco Osuna (*c.* 1000 AD)

When any object is subjected to a load it may become deformed in some way. If on removing the load the object resumes its original shape it is said to be elastic; if it remains deformed it is called plastic. Thus an elastic band is so called because it will return to its original shape when released. But if you were to stretch it too far then it might remain permanently stretched to some extent. When this occurs it is said to have exceeded its limit of elasticity.

A similar phenomenon takes place with the human body. When it is put under some load the physiology may be changed in a number of different ways. If the changes are only slight the body will be able to return to what is known as the state of 'homeostatic balance': a state in which all the variables are in mutual equilibrium. But if the variables are displaced too far they may exceed the 'limit of homeostatic tolerance': they will not return to the ideal norm but stay slightly displaced. We could say that the physiology has ceased to be perfectly elastic and has remained a little 'stretched'. The overloading experience has left a physiological scar, and the body is said to have accumulated stress. (If we were to follow the physicists' definition then we should say that the body has accumulated strain. Stress is the load displacing the variables while strain is the effect. The biological sciences are however looser than the physical sciences in this respect and often refer to the effect as a stress. Since Maharishi also uses stress in this looser sense it will be less confusing, even if less pedantic, if I use the word 'stress' to refer to the physiological changes occurring within the organism in response to some external load.)

There are many factors which can give rise to human stress. At the physical level it is produced by electric shock, intense heat or cold, physical wounds, loud noises, malnutrition, lack of sleep, physical exhaustion, drugs, etc. On the psychological level the mere threat of any of these can be a stress. The loss of personal or social esteem, the deflation of the ego, and anything which upsets or threatens to upset one's sense of identity will likewise be a source of stress. Demanding jobs, jobs which do not demand enough, responsibilities that one cannot cope with, extreme competition, overcrowding, conflicting personal and social goals, continual adaptation to opposing social pressures, and mental fatigue are also common forms of stress.

It is now thought by many psychologists that change itself can be a stress. It has been observed that a large proportion of illnesses occur during or immediately after significant changes in a person's life. The death of a close friend or loved one, changing jobs and moving house all correlate highly with illness and stress.[1]

As stress continues to build up the perception becomes duller and less sensitive with the result that the effects of further stress become less noticeable and only the heavier overloads reach consciousness. Hardly noticing the damage being incurred, the heavily stressed person charges into situations from which a less stressed, more sensitive individual would quickly withdraw. And the more stressed that a person becomes the weaker the body becomes and the less it is able to cope with further overloads. We become trapped in a vicious circle – or rather a vicious spiral – winding ourselves up until, like a weak elastic band which has been stretched too far, too often, we snap! We break down, mentally and physically.

The Flight-Fight Response

Physical evolution is, by our standards of time, a very slow process. The human body is developing no faster today than it did a million years ago. But our minds, our knowledge of the world, and our ability to manipulate the environment are changing far more rapidly. In these fields humanity has progressed more in the last few hundred years than it did in all of its preceding million years taken together. As a consequence we are now living in a twentieth-century environment, with (it is hoped) twentieth-century minds, yet with bodies that have not changed significantly since the stone age.

There is one physiological mechanism in particular which is something of a hangover from the past. It was first recognized in 1929 by an American physiologist called Walter Cannon who named it the 'Flight-Fight Response'. As its name suggests it is a preparation for fleeing or fighting and is invoked whenever there is a threat of danger. The effect is an immediate mustering of all the body's resources in preparation for intense activity.

The response is said to be both integrated and stereotyped: integrated in that all, or nearly all, the organs of the body are involved, each modifying their functioning so as to be of the greatest value in the impending activity; and stereotyped in that a very wide variety of stimuli will all elicit this same basic response – in fact it can be triggered by almost any form of threat, psychological as well as physical.

Much of the brain's control of the body is affected by the discharge of hormones. These are chemical messengers which travel round the body activating or inactivating various organs. Whenever there is a threat of danger specific hormones are released in abundance into the bloodstream. Their effect is to change temporarily the functioning of the whole body. The heart speeds up, blood pressure rises, the lungs take in more oxygen, the muscles become tense, fats and sugars are released into the blood to provide more energy, and the body begins to cool itself through perspiration. At the same time digestion, sexual activities and other processes which will not be needed come to a halt. In short the organism becomes instantly mobilized.

Several thousand years ago when one was completely at the mercy of the surroundings, this flight-fight response was undoubt-edly very useful. If you met with some wild animal then your very survival might depend on the ability instantly to prepare yourself for activity. You either had to flee, or, if cornered, fight the animal. You could not just stand there. Today, however, the response has lost much of its survival value. Urban man seldom encounters situations where he has either to run for his life or fight to the death, and the response has become more of a handicap than an advantage.

Imagine that you are walking down a street and a car suddenly speeds by very close. You feel startled and alarmed. It makes you 'jump', but only mentally. What has happened physiologically is that the speeding car has signified possible danger and set off the flight–fight response. Your heart beats faster, blood pressure increases, you sweat a little, and your muscles tense. But you do not run away, nor do you fight the car. You continue walking down the street and only gradually does the reaction subside.

If you think that pedestrians get a raw deal, pause for a moment to consider the driver of a car. Experiments have shown that the city driver is in a continual state of physiological arousal. When overtaking another vehicle, for instance, the heart rate may rise to 150 or 160 beats per minute, blood pressure increases, the palms sweat and the muscles tense, as one prepares oneself for no greater activity than a slight movement of the wrists and ankle. Half an hour in city traffic will usually leave a person in a state of hyper-arousal from which it may take several hours to recover.

But it is not only physical dangers which will produce this response. Any threat to one's sense of identity will invoke the same response. If you are insulted, for example, then the blood pressure will again rise, the heart starts pounding, the muscles tense, and the face flushes perhaps. You feel as if you could hit the person – but usually you restrain yourself and try to 'simmer down'.

Most of us probably regard it as almost a matter of definition that a stress is something 'distressful' and unpleasant. But pleasant stimuli can also be a source of stress if they overload the nervous system. To win a lottery, for example, would almost certainly be a pleasant experience but it might also produce a similar adverse physiological reaction to those of an unpleasant experience. Most of us have had such excitement at some time. Often we describe the event by saying that 'the heart leapt with joy'. But it is this very 'leaping' of the physiological processes that culminates in stress. Lennart Levi, an eminent stress researcher from the Karolinski Institute in Stockholm, has supported this view by showing that amusing and laughter-provoking films elicit the same kind of physiological reaction characteristic of stress as do aggressive or horror films.[2]

A milder form of the flight–fight reaction known as the 'alerting response' occurs every time there is some major or significant change in the surroundings. A sudden noise, for example, will make the ears 'prick up', the head turn, and the eyes focus in the direction of the sound. One is ready, should there be any danger, to go into a full-blown flight–fight reaction.

In every case the flight–fight response prepares the body for action, yet almost invariably we do not act and do not play out the reaction to its intended end. We remain doing whatever it was that we were doing, perhaps just sitting at a desk, yet with a body prepared and yearning for action. The tense muscles are not used, the fats and sugars in the blood are not consumed, and the physiology stays displaced. After a quarter of an hour or so you may feel that you are back to normal. But do not be deceived. Although the hormonal changes which started the response may not last very long it may well be an hour or more before the body has completely returned to normal.

If this just happens occasionally then perhaps there is little harm, but when it happens continually the situation is very different. Imagine this reaction setting in every fifteen minutes. Not only do you never play out the reaction but you never even recover from one alert before the next one sets in. A state of *continual* physiological arousal and tension results. Blood pressure remains high, the blood-chemistry stays changed, the muscles continue to be tense and we feel 'wound up'.

This permanent imbalance leads to many functional disturbances in the body. Layer upon layer of fat is deposited on the walls of the arteries choking them and precipitating heart failure. The natural balance of acids in the stomach is upset and it begins literally to digest itself resulting in peptic ulcers. Skin disorders such as eczema result from the abnormal chemical secretions in the skin. The lungs, kidneys, bladder, reproductive system, muscles, eyes and brain are all susceptible to similar damage.

Nor is the damage purely physical. As stress accumulates there is a general loss of vitality. The continuous over-stimulation and physiological hyper-arousal raises the level of background activity in the mind, effectively raising the threshold for conscious experience. What was before a quiet level of conscious thought is submerged by the increased mental noise and disappears from the conscious mind. Thinking becomes less clear, less resourceful and less efficient. We feel dull, 'under the weather', or 'off colour'. The body is sluggish to respond and our actions become inept and ineffective.

One might suppose that the remedy would be to engage in vigorous exercise every time that the reaction was aroused. Undoubtedly the problem of stress has been made worse by our tendency to lead more sedentary lives, but exercise alone will not solve the problem. In many cases of alarm such action would be most inappropriate. Our society does not condone the person who starts a fight at the slightest provocation. The city driver could hardly jump out of the car and run for his life every time another car came too close. And the aspiring executive who did fifty press-ups every time a phone call or news bulletin threatened his career would probably lose his job anyway.

The pace of life today is such that there is just not enough time to allow the body to readjust. Indeed, as time goes on, the pace of life speeds up, subjecting us to more and more change, and, if we fail to adapt, to more and more stress. Fifteen years hence the pace of life will probably be double what it is now, and the level of stress many times higher. It is therefore imperative that we find a way to adapt faster and cope with the stress as soon as possible.

Rest – The Release of Stress

What is particularly novel in Maharishi's teaching on stress is his clear insistence that the accumulation of stress can be reversed; that given the chance the body will automatically dissolve accumulated physical tensions and return towards the optimum homeostatic balance. And, claims Maharishi, the condition which allows this reversal to take place is simply the condition of deep rest.

When in physics a load is applied to an object the work done by the load produces some structural change in the object and this change represents an increase in potential energy. When the physical system is 'relaxed' this energy is converted back into kinetic energy – hence the effectiveness of an elastic band as a catapult. What Maharishi is saying is that the same principles apply to human physiology.

When stress is being accumulated abnormal activity produces some physical change in the organism, representing a gain in potential energy. Work has had to be done against the body's natural tendency to return to a state of homeostatic equilibrium. When stress is being dissolved the reverse takes place. The energy stored in the stress is released resulting in some temporary increase of activity in the organism.

This activity could take many forms depending on the stress that is being released. In many cases it will not even be noticed. Sometimes the dissolution of the stress may produce some increase in brain activity. In this case the change would be experienced as some random thought or mental image suddenly popping up into the mind.

Now one might expect that in this situation the thought which appeared would be closely related to the original stressful experience. But this is not the case. What determines the meaning and content of a thought is the present state of the brain. All the dissolving stress has done is to increase temporarily the mental activity: it does not by itself determine the thought which will be generated. It may, however, determine in a very general way the type of thought that occurred.

If, for example, a stress had been caused by some strong visual experience then this will probably have left some permanent traces in the associated areas of the nervous system. On being dissolved there will therefore be some increased activity in these areas and, provided that it reached consciousness, this would give rise to a visual experience. But the overall state of the brain will have changed considerably over the period between the inception and the dissolution of the stress and so the actual content, meaning and details of the present experience will almost certainly bear little relationship to the original stress.

It is probable that similar processes are happening during normal sleep, our nightly dreams signifying the release of some tension somewhere in the system. Maharishi believes that since the TM technique provides a much deeper form of rest than is normally gained during sleep it is able to dissolve more deeply rooted stresses. But the TM technique should not be seen as a replacement for sleep. Although many people do find that as a result of the practice they do not need as much sleep as before, this is not the prime intention of the TM program. To give the body this extra rest at the expense of sleep would be counterproductive. The real value of the TM technique lies in its ability to restore the balance between rest and activity and thereby enrich all aspects of life.

People often wonder whether the total elimination of stress would be beneficial. Una Kroll, for example, in her appraisal of the TM technique feels that a fully relaxed person would not be able to do well in examinations, interviews or public speaking. She argues that[3]: 'It is only under the stimulus of the audience that the speaker really comes alive.' Her difficulty would seem to stem from two different uses of the word 'stress'. The physicist talks of stress as the pressure being applied, whereas the biologist talks of it as the physiological reaction to this pressure. Una Kroll is saying that we all need pressure to draw out the best in us, and with this I would certainly agree – if the audience is not demanding, the exam of no consequence, or the interview unimportant there would be little incentive to apply oneself wholeheartedly to the task. But this should not be confused with stress in the sense of physiological damage which is invariably an impediment to effective thought and action. From my own experience it is only when one is calm and rested that one can think clearly, draw deeply upon one's knowledge and experience, and present it in a coherent and comprehensive manner.

What is necessary is not physiological stress but the ability to respond effectively to a demanding situation without simultaneously driving the body into a state of imbalance. In the physicist's terms we need the stress without the strain. So the release of physiological tension which the TM technique provides, far from being a handicap in these situations, would be a distinct advantage.

Another point which should be made clear is that a stress is not the same as a memory. When the body throws off some stress it is simply throwing off the undesirable side-effects arising from an inability in the past to cope with a certain experience. We in no way lose the memory of that experience or all that we have learnt from it.

The Stay and Play Response

The flight–fight response is controlled by what is known as the sympathetic nervous system. Complementing this is the parasympathetic nervous system which when activated promotes the conservation of energy. It facilitates digestive processes, reduces heart rate and lowers blood pressure. Ideally the body should be balanced between sympathetic and parasympathetic activity, changing from one to the other as the situation demands. Unfortunately the person who is in a permanent state of tension remains overbalanced in the direction of sympathetic arousal. The TM technique appears to redress this balance by eliciting a parasympathetic response which lowers heart rate, blood pressure, muscle tension, etc., and appears to be the exact opposite of the flight–fight response.

Whereas the flight–fight response is brought on by fear the relaxation response characteristic of the TM technique is brought on by the increasing enjoyment experienced as the mind settles down into quieter levels of thinking. This has led Dr David Orme-Johnson to dub it the 'stay and play' response.

Orme-Johnson studied the rate of occurrence of small electrical changes in the skin known as the galvanic skin response (GSR). These fluctuations occur most frequently when a person is startled in some way and accompany the flight–fight response. He found that when he repeatedly made a subject 'jump' by sounding a loud tone, those who practised the TM technique quickly habituated (i.e. the skin response ceased to occur) while the non-meditators continued to react each time they heard the sound.[4] This suggested that they had gained some greater resilience to stress. It also indicated that the meditator might be becoming more stable both in himself and in his interactions with others. Previously it had been found that people who displayed a high frequency of spontaneous GSRs tended to be introverted, unstable, anxious and prone to mental and physical illness. Conversely those in whom these fluctuations were relatively fewer tended to be more stable – both physiologically and emotionally – better able to relate to the surroundings, and more mature.

Dr Denver Daniels working at Exeter University has taken this work further. He studied the GSR response of meditators and non-meditators subjected to unpleasant noises – the sound of finger nails scraping down a blackboard. This was a large-scale study involving some 200 subjects of which one-third were regularly practising the TM technique. The 120 or so non-meditators showed the expected sudden drop in GSR, slowly returning to normal over a period of about five minutes. The meditators on the other hand recovered much more quickly, and the longer they had been practising the TM technique the faster the recovery. In those who had been practising the technique for several years there was often no reaction whatsoever to the unpleasant noise. This was not because they had not heard it – they reported that it was indeed a most unpleasant noise – but they were no longer showing the same adverse physiological reaction to it, i.e. the flight–fight reaction was no longer being evoked.[5]

This work suggests that those practising the TM technique were indeed increasing their resistance to stress. Furthermore, it suggests that they were able to adapt faster to a changing environment. In his book *Future Shock*, Alvin Toffler argues that the pace of life is continually speeding up and that man is rapidly approaching the state where he can no longer adapt fast enough to the ever-increasing changes in his environment. What man needs, concludes Toffler, is to find some means by which he can increase his adaptability. These experiments suggest that the TM program may well be a way.

Health, Creativity and Intelligence

7

The so-called normal man, the one we may term the 'healthy Philistine', is only a fraction of what he could be.

William James

Over two thousand years ago Plato wrote that: 'The cure of the part should not be attempted without the treatment of the whole ... and therefore if the head and body are to be well, you must begin by curing the mind: that is the first thing.' Western medicine has progressed considerably since Plato. We know how to cut the body open and adjust its parts when it goes wrong; how and where most diseases attack us; and how to stave off these attacks with drugs of one kind or another.

But despite all these advances we are only just beginning to appreciate the root causes of many of these disorders and still tend to regard the body more as a machine than an organism. In this respect we appear to have progressed very little since Plato's time.

When we fall ill we are often more concerned with removing the symptoms of the problem than its root cause. Once we 'feel' well again we consider ourselves no longer in need of any care. But the physical symptoms which we are so keen to eliminate are generally only the tip of the iceberg. Cutting off its top is no solution for the iceberg immediately bobs up to reveal more of itself. Submerging the iceberg will keep it out of sight so long as you keep it down, but as soon as you let it go it will come bobbing up again. Rather than just trying to remove or suppress the physical symptoms, medicine should be equally concerned with treating the root cause of the disorders.

Now what is the root cause? A decade ago doctors were cautiously proposing that perhaps 50 per cent of all disorders were caused by stress. This figure grew rapidly and in 1972 Peter Blythe started his book *Stress Disease* with the statement 'Authoritative medical opinion in the United States and Britain has gone on record to the effect that up to 70 per cent of all patients currently being treated by doctors in general practice are suffering from conditions which have their origins in unrelieved stress.' Two years later Dr Elmer Green speaking at a conference on health in London remarked that[1] 'even stuffy doctors are now agreeing that 80 per cent of all problems are psychosomatic.' Some less 'stuffy' doctors would suggest that the figure is probably higher still.

We saw in the last chapter how stress could be a major factor in the incidence of peptic ulcers, high blood pressure, coronary problems, etc., and most of us would also accept that many of our incidental aches and pains are also a product of stress. But what about infectious diseases, these surely are not caused by stress but by bacteria and viruses? That is true, but the body's susceptibility to bacterial or viral attack depends upon the person's overall health; the less stressed person is less likely to fall ill in the first place and better able to cope with any illnesses that do occur. There is now mounting evidence that even the incidence of many forms of cancer is closely related to the patient's emotional state; frequently it has been found that the appearance of the disease follows a serious emotional loss occurring six to eighteen months earlier.[2]

Just in terms of the stress relief which the TM technique provides we should therefore expect a general improvement in health amongst meditators. It is getting to the root cause of many disorders and, by treating the mind and body together as an integrated unit, is fulfilling the Platonic ideal of medicine. People practising the TM technique have often reported that they feel healthier, and some preliminary surveys are beginning to substantiate these claims, showing not only a general improvement in health but a corresponding decrease in the use of tranquillizers and other medicinal drugs.[3]

The TM Program in Psychotherapy

It is not only physical health that is improved. A New York psychiatrist who started using the TM program as an adjunct to conventional psychotherapy reported that:[4]

> [those] who have persevered with TM have shown a much faster rate of improvement in the course of psychotherapy. With several this improvement has been dramatic, even spectacular. Some have been relieved of symptoms that had never been helped by psychotherapy. With two such patients this relief and general improvement, increase in ego-strength, general productivity at work and happiness in living have continued with greatly decreased hours of psychotherapy. With every patient who has been faithful in TM, the improvement has been at least twice the expected rate (as judged by previous experience with the patient). Sometimes it seems to be at least ten times the expected rate. Sometimes when a patient complains about not moving at a satisfactory rate I find that the patient has stopped TM. When TM is again undertaken, movement picks up again.

Dr Bernard Glueck from the Hartford Institute of Living in Connecticut has been using the TM program for some time in his treatment of schizophrenia. His findings are very encouraging. He gave a third of his group the TM technique, a third biofeedback training and a third a standard relaxation technique. His results show the TM technique to be the most effective of the three, most of the meditating patients being able to cut down considerably on conventional medication.[5] The TM program had the advantage over biofeedback of not requiring elaborate and expensive equipment. With the biofeedback patients he found that positive results were only obtained so long as they had access to the EEG and computer: they could not relax on their own as the TM subjects could.

Dr Harold Bloomfield, who has also used the TM program as part of his psychiatric practice, notes several other advantages of the practice over drugs and therapists. The TM technique is exclusively under the control of the patient. If he gets better it is not due to a pill or a therapist but to his own natural regenerative processes. In addition the TM program saves time both for the doctor and for the patient.[6] Many of his patients reported that since starting the TM technique psychosomatic diseases such as skin rashes, muscle tension, stomach pains and headaches were disappearing, and they were generally enjoying a new lease of life, with increased stability and happiness.[7]

Two particularly interesting cases in which the TM program appears to have brought about remarkable personal changes are described by Daniel Goleman in the *Journal of Transpersonal Psychology*.[8] The first involved a woman in her late forties who had obviously suffered a great degree of distress over her mother's death, to which she had never grown fully accustomed. During one TM session much of this latent sadness, which had been locked up within, flowed out. Afterwards she not only regained many of the happy memories of her childhood which previously had been suppressed, but she also began to see people 'as though for the first time ... like all the grey cardboard figures came to life'. She continued:

> Had you asked me yesterday, I would have felt my percep-
> tion was excellent, but I have been perceiving people
> through learned responses ... not *seeing* them. All that is
> different now ... when I saw my daughters' faces I really
> saw them like I hadn't ever before, and they knew, they
> responded.

In view of the stressed conditions in which many of us live it is particularly interesting to note that she did not realize beforehand that she was not functioning to her full capacity. Until the 'doors of perception' are cleansed there is little awareness of the grey fog through which everything is seen, and it comes as a surprise to many, although a pleasant surprise, to discover that awareness can be sharper, richer and more lively.

In the previous chapter we saw that the actual form of the stress dissolution process bears little relation to the original stressful experience. This is clearly illustrated in the case of this woman. Although she experienced some of the feelings connected with her mother's death, she did not relive that past experience. Psychoanalytic approaches to mental health often attempt to eliminate the stressful effects of past experience by bringing the forgotten or suppressed experiences back into consciousness. This is in sharp contrast to the TM technique where there is never any attempt to delve into the past. In this respect Maharishi is going against the predominant psychoanalytic view which holds that only a full awareness of the original cause will allow the person to cope with the stress.

This difference between the TM program and conventional psychotherapy is important for Maharishi. If one deliberately relives the experience there is the danger that the conscious recall of the experience might itself result in further stress. By innocently allowing the tension to flow out without going through the original disturbance the meditator is not adversely affected by the process.

The second case which Goleman quotes in his article is particularly remarkable in that it involves the normalization of a physical deformity. It concerns a girl of twenty-two, who reports:

> I had very crooked teeth when I was a child. My teeth are so big for my jaw they had to pull eight teeth. When my second teeth came, I started to notice my jaws didn't match. For several months while I meditated I would feel my jaw pulling around, always to the right. It got more and more intense, and then the other day there was a very strong and painful pull, a large 'Crack!' and my jaw moved over. When it happened I was so amazed, it was so intense, but I didn't stop meditating, I knew what was happening. When I looked in the mirror, my teeth were aligned.
>
> Now my mouth muscles are more relaxed; when I smile now it feels different.

I know of a similar case concerning a young man who had broken his elbow in a motor accident two years previously. Although it had mended fairly well he could not completely straighten his arm. His doctors told him this was a fairly common occurrence resulting from the way the bone had reset. They added that it was impossible to do anything about it and he would have to put up with it as a permanent disability. However, two years later, during a TM session he suddenly had an intense pain in the elbow very similar to the pain of the accident. At the same time his hand became paralysed again. A surgeon who examined him during this episode confirmed that the paralysis was of the same form as that which would be caused by an injury to the nerve at the elbow. Two days later the pain had disappeared and so had the restriction of the elbow. He was now able to straighten his arm as fully as anyone else.

Most people would be prepared to accept that some forms of mental and emotional damage are reversible, but the idea that physical structural damage could also be reversible is astonishing. Many doctors would doubt whether such changes are possible without major surgery let alone concede that they could occur spontaneously as they did in these cases.

Of course, experiences such as these do not happen every time one practises the technique; they happen only occasionally. But even their occasional occurrence is of profound import for medical science. If it could be substantiated that such reversibility were possible on a much wider scale it would herald a revolution not only in medical practice but in our whole understanding of the human organism.

The Expansion of the Mind

William James, one of the fathers of twentieth-century psychology, recorded that:

> most people live, whether physically, intellectually or morally, in a very restricted circle of their potential being. They make use of a very small portion of their possible consciousness ... much like a man, who, out of his whole bodily organism, should get into the habit of using and moving only his little finger.

Many other psychologists have expressed similar views, saying that most of us use only 10 per cent of our full potential. Whether the figure is 10 per cent or not is questionable – 10 per cent is probably a generous overestimate – but whatever the figure is, it is certainly small.

In Maharishi's model of the mind we are only aware of the surface levels of mental activity. Mental stresses maintain the background neural activity at a high level, preventing one from being aware of the quieter underlying levels of thinking. In terms of the pond analogy, the effects of stress are like mud in the water. The bubble is seen only at the surface because the water below is murky. But if the water were to become clearer we could begin to see it rising up from the depths of the pond. As the nervous system becomes freer from stress the background of mental 'chatter' decreases and ordinary thoughts are appreciated at earlier and earlier stages in their development, not only during the Transcendental Meditation technique but in daily activity as well. The proportion of mental activity which reaches consciousness increases until, when the system is completely free from stress, the whole of mental activity is open to consciousness. Maharishi refers to this as 'an expansion of the conscious capacity of the mind'.

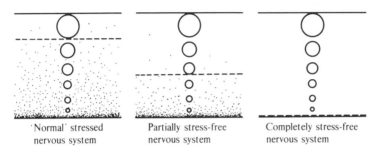

'Normal' stressed nervous system

Partially stress-free nervous system

Completely stress-free nervous system

– – – – – Effective threshold for conscious experience

Figure 8   *Expansion of conscious capacity of the mind: lowering of effective threshold for conscious experience with progressive dissolution of stress.*

This expansion of the conscious mind does not mean that one actually experiences one's mind becoming larger or anything like that: it is simply that the finer levels of thinking are now open to the awareness and one begins to make more use of these in normal thinking. What one actually experiences is thinking becoming clearer, faster and more effective.

Maharishi talks of thinking at these subtler levels being more powerful. He is not suggesting that mental activity becomes more intense – that would clearly contradict the notion of subtler thought levels: what he is saying is that thinking at subtler levels has more potential and is more effective. We might liken the situation to driving with the car radio on. When speeding down the freeway the noise of the engine and the wind necessitate turning the radio up full and what we hear is only the general outline of the music, the rest is either distorted or drowned out. When we slow down we can turn the radio down and we then find that many of the subtleties of the music become apparent. Similarly with thinking, at quieter levels of activity much of the subtlety of thought is revealed and thinking becomes far richer, and when translated into action, that much more effective.

The reduction in background noise also has a marked effect on perception and activity. The brain might be considered as an immensely complex decision-making system. Each neuron is receiving signals from hundreds, perhaps thousands, of other cells. Some of these pulses may be meaningful signals or they may be unwanted 'noise'. One job of the brain is to sort out the signals from the noise in order that it can decide how best to respond. The more noise there is the harder will this task be. To take a specific example, we can in a quiet room distinguish two notes which are only very slightly different. But if there were a pneumatic drill outside the window most of us would probably be unable to distinguish the two. Because of the other noise, in this case external noise, the brain no longer has sufficient information with which to make a decision. The two 'sound the same'. Similar decision-making processes govern nearly every process in the brain. Thus the fineness of our perception and the delicacy of our actions depend in part on the degree to which we can detect minute differences in internal signals, and this in turn depends upon the amount of noise in the system.

In addition to the personal reports of many meditators several different lines of psychological research indicate that there is a general increased sensitivity amongst TM subjects. Graham,[9] Pirot,[10] and Brown *et al.*,[11] have all found significant improvements in perception. Shaw and Kolb[12] found that the reaction time of meditators was faster than non-meditators, and Blasdell[13] found that TM subjects were more accurate in complex eye–hand co-ordination tasks. In fact, since nearly everything we do is mediated by the ability of the nervous system to make fine discriminations one would expect a decrease in neural noise to lead to some improvement in nearly every field of activity.

Intelligence

The sharper perception, clearer thinking and more efficient action that is claimed to come with the TM program might be expected to lead to an increase in intelligence. Maharishi claims that this is indeed the case, but when he uses the word intelligence he is using it in a special sense. He defines intelligence as that which gives order and direction to change. So when he talks of a person becoming more intelligent he means that thinking and action are becoming more orderly. Thus, as far as Maharishi is concerned, the more intelligent person is he who is better able to order his perceptual data into meaningful form and direct his activity in a more effective direction.

This concept is, in fact, in keeping with modern approaches to the study of intelligence which are now moving away from the idea of intelligence as a fixed constant such as IQ and looking at it more in terms of a person's ability to learn as a result of experience; to abstract the common elements from situations which may appear to have little in common, and to apply them to future activities.

Although there is not the space here to discuss the matter fully, several lines of research suggest that the TM technique results in an increase in both the speed and capacity of information-processing in the brain, changes which we might expect to lead to an increase in intelligence.[14] Tests in Holland have given further support to this contention. Measuring a factor known as the 'intelligence growth rate' it was found that schoolchildren practising the TM technique increased significantly compared with a similar non-meditating control group.[15]

Maharishi sees an increased orderliness of thinking to be the result of an increased orderliness in brain activity (illustrated by the increase in synchrony and coherence of the EEG patterns), and claims that this orderliness is itself a direct consequence of giving the nervous system deep rest. He writes:[16]

> This rule of 'intelligence through rest' seems to be analogous to a very general law of nature discovered by the science of physics to apply to all natural systems.
>
> This law, the third law of thermodynamics, states that entropy (disorder) decreases when temperature (activity) decreases and that the condition of zero entropy, perfect orderliness, coincides with a temperature of absolute zero (absolutely no activity). In fact, the region near absolute zero temperature in physical systems is closely connected with a strong tendency towards wave coherence and synchrony and is exemplified in the onset of superfluidity and superconductivity near absolute zero temperature when activity is minimum. This suggests a striking analogy to the synchrony of brain waves induced by the very deep rest of TM. If we

define for the purpose of comparison a 'mental temperature', corresponding to the level of mental and neurophysiological activity, and systematically reduce this through the technique of TM, we perceive a class of tendencies in the human mind that reminds us of the third law as seen in the realm of basic physics. This quantum mechanical analogy suggests that orderliness in the brain and in thinking is natural to man. TM accomplishes this orderliness by providing an opportunity for the mind to follow the natural tendency of the most general patterns of nature.

This idea that the tendency towards increased orderliness is a natural impulse of life was also recognized by the physicist Erwin Schrödinger. 'Life,' he wrote,[17] 'feeds upon negative entropy'. If an organism's total entropy were to increase then it would pass into a state of molecular disorder characteristic of death. A creature stays alive because it is able to 'drink' order from its environment and remain in a highly ordered state. Following Maharishi, we could say that life was therefore the expression of intelligence in Nature, and that by reducing mental activity the TM technique enables the individual to drink more fully of orderliness and of life itself.

Creativity

Creativity is generally thought of as the ability to produce novel and original change and usually involves some association or synthesis of previously unassociated concepts. Newton, watching an apple fall, made an association between the motion of the apple and the orbit of the moon and created his theory of gravity. Shakespeare set private love against public duty in *Antony and Cleopatra*, and Cézanne brought the diverse elements of a setting and their underlying oneness together in his paintings.

Many creative people, both scientists and artists alike, have noted that creative thinking most frequently takes place when the mind is in a quiet relaxed state. Kekulé, for instance, solved the problem of the shape of the benzene molecule – a problem which was baffling many chemists of his day – whilst idly day-dreaming in front of his fire. And Coleridge, as every student knows, composed the Kubla Khan while in a dream.

In terms of Maharishi's model of the mind the dream state

corresponds to a subtler level of thinking. Subtler levels of thought are by definition less structured and less well-defined than the grosser levels of thought and the more the boundaries dissolve the more chance there is of making cross-connections. The associations made in such states have still to be put in a more concrete form so the creative person tends to be someone who can alternate between the deeper states of reverie and the surface waking state.

In so far as the TM technique takes the attention to deeper levels of the mind than usually reached during dreaming it affords the possibility of making more fundamental and further reaching cross-connections. It is a common experience that on finishing a TM session one often finds the solution to a problem that had been on the mind for a long time. No attempt is made during the practice to find solutions to problems – that would almost certainly keep the attention on the surface levels of thought and out of meditation: the association is made quite spontaneously and without conscious direction.

Moreover, by expanding the conscious capacity of the mind, the TM program allows one to retain an awareness of the deeper levels of thought while in the waking state. So creative thought begins to become a more general feature of life, occurring throughout the waking state as well as in states of deep reverie.

We could also look at the creative process in terms of the two hemispheres of the brain. There is some evidence that creative thought is associated with the right side of the brain. Yet the creative person must still make full use of the left side as well. An intuitive insight is no good if it cannot be formulated and communicated. The creative person is thus one who can both make spontaneous cross-connections and then develop a verbal or symbolic expression of that synthesis. This integration is enhanced by the type of brain synchrony observed during the TM technique, and the fact that this continues afterwards again suggests that the technique should lead to a general increase in creativity. This hypothesis has been borne out in tests of meditators which do indeed show higher creativity,[18] and the greater their EEG coherence the greater their increase in creativity.[19]

With regard to artistic creativity in particular it has sometimes been suggested that any reduction in stress would lead to a reduction in creativity. It is said that many great works of art have been created by people under considerable stress and that this stress was necessary for their creativity. If all stress were to be released there would no longer be any incentive for artistic expression.

In answering this objection Maharishi concedes that some 'spur' is needed in order for an artist to create – all activity needs a spur or incentive – but, he says, it is not necessary that this spur be one of stress. If all stress is eliminated then any incentive for creative activity will be able to flow forth that much more freely.

In essence he is making the same distinction between stress as pressure and stress as physiological damage that I pointed out in the previous chapter. The artist needs stress in the sense of pressure, but not in the sense of physiological disorders. If the artist's nervous system is not strong enough to cope with the demands made of it then the pressure needed for creative work may well result in some physiological damage. Maharishi's point is that although such physiological stress may, for most artists, be an inevitable consequence of their work it is not a necessary prerequisite for it. Creativity depends upon having a heightened awareness, an openness of mind, and the ability to resolve inner discords through a creative synthesis. These are all abilities which a reduction in physiological stress would enhance.

Water the Root!

Maharishi maintains that most problems arise as a result of stress, and that the TM technique by releasing stress is effectively getting to the root of all problems. This should not be taken to imply that the TM technique alone will instantly solve everything. Many problems are the result of very real physical difficulties and these will only be resolved by action of some kind on the physical level. Maharishi's point is that merely attending to the surface symptoms of the problem without simultaneously tending to the root of the problem, will never offer a complete solution.

Maharishi likens the process of meditation to that of a gardener tending a sick bush. The leaves of the bush may be withering, changing colour, or ailing in some other way, but if the gardener were to tend only to these surface symptoms of the problem he would not get very far. The solution that any competent gardener would take is simply to supply the correct nourishment to the root and let nature take care of the whole process in her own efficient way.

Much of our time we spend tending to the leaves rather than the root of our problems. We see countless difficulties around us; some personal, others social, political, economic, educational or environmental. Faced with such an abundance of problems the common reaction is to pick out the most urgent or least difficult one and charge ahead at finding a solution. But more often than not this is only eliminating the symptoms of a much deeper problem. We would be much more effective if simultaneously we were to attend to the root of the problem, and in many cases the root is individual stress.

Maharishi sums this up with the phrase, 'Water the root to enjoy the fruit'. But notice how he says '. . . *to* enjoy the fruit'. He does not merely remark '. . . *and* enjoy the fruit', which would make the enjoyment something of a side-effect. He emphasizes that the ultimate purpose of meditation lies not in the experience of finer levels of thinking, the rest, the release of stress or the development of Creative Intelligence, but in the enjoyment which naturally follows as a result of all these. It is this personal fulfilment which makes it all worth while.

Part Two

Part One looked briefly at the historical origins of the TM technique and the growth of Maharishi's movement in the world today. We considered the technique itself, how it allows one to experience quieter levels of the normal thinking process and why it is so important that no effort or control enters into the practice. We then saw what the observable effects of the TM program were; how the brain was beginning to function more efficiently and how the body was coming to a deep state of rest, dissolving stress and tension built up in the past. This section ended by looking at the implications of this for health and individual development.

Now I want to turn and consider the effects that these changes in physiology and brain functioning have on the way in which we perceive and appreciate both ourselves and the world around us. Part Two will be looking at the different states of consciousness to which the TM program can lead and how these help the individual integrate with the world around him and start living a life of fulfilment. In this section of the book many of Maharishi's points are illustrated with similar points from other teachings, past and present, and the closing chapters of this section look at the type of distortions which have crept into such teachings in the past and how today the teaching is being set on a much firmer basis through the establishment of the Maharishi International University.

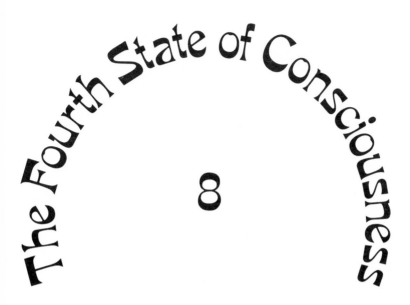

The Fourth State of Consciousness

8

Look, it cannot be seen – it is beyond form
Listen, it cannot be heard – it is beyond sound
Grasp, it cannot be held – it is intangible

Tao-Te-Ching

Throughout the practice of the Transcendental Meditation technique one is wide awake. Even when one transcends the finest level of mental activity and arrives at the state of restful alertness one still remains conscious. In this state of quiet all mental activity has died away. Consciousness has ceased to vibrate and there is no longer anything to be conscious of. The normal thinking activity of the mind has been transcended, and for this reason the state is known as *transcendental consciousness.*

But although consciousness has ceased to vibrate it has not ceased to exist: it simply does not take on a specific form. The state is not therefore one of unconsciousness so much as un-manifest or pure consciousness. Since consciousness itself remains, the subject of all experience, the experiencer, also remains. Thus we might also call the state one of pure self. But this pure self is not, as we shall see later in this chapter, the ego, or any other form of individual identity, for all these 'selves' are concepts or constructs of the mind, products of mental activity, and as such they die when mental activity dies. The pure self is fundamental to all experience. Being the very basis of experience, it continues to exist even though there may no longer be anything to experience. In order to distinguish these two uses of the word 'self' I shall follow the practice of referring to the individual empirical self as the self, and to the pure self, the qualityless subject of all experience, as the Self with a capital 'S'.

The Fourth State of Consciousness

The state of transcendental consciousness is quite distinct from the three commonly encountered states of consciousness, waking, dreaming and deep sleep. We may allocate these three major states of consciousness to the squares of a simple 2 × 2 matrix, each square being uniquely specified by two parameters: (1) whether or not the subject is awake; and (2) whether or not the subject is aware of anything. When we do this then transcendental consciousness fits very neatly into the fourth square of the table.

	Awake	Asleep
Objects of consciousness	Waking	Dreaming
No objects of consciousness	Transcendental state	Deep sleep

Figure 9   *A fourth major state of consciousness.*

This classification of the states of consciousness is, of course, only a very generalized one. Besides the many shades of consciousness within the waking, dreaming and deep sleep states there are also the borderline regions where one state merges into the other. Nevertheless, this scheme is useful as a very general basis for distinguishing the transcendental state from each of the other three.

We can gain some insight into the relationship of these four states of consciousness by likening them to the different ways in which we can see a cinema screen. In this analogy the cinema projector corresponds to the brain projecting images on to the 'screen of the mind'. According to what is happening in the 'projector' many different scenes can be perceived on the 'screen'.

If the cinema projector were to be connected to some outside broadcast camera then we would see on the screen various real-life situations as they occurred. This corresponds to the ordinary waking state of consciousness in which we are more or less directly aware of the outside world.

If a film of some kind is being shown by the projector, then whatever appears on the screen, whether it be a replay of past events, a thriller, a cartoon, or merely abstract images, will usually bear little relation to what is happening outside the theatre. This corresponds to the dreaming state of consciousness in which memories and fantasies enter our awareness.

When the projector is switched off, leaving everything in darkness, the situation is similar to deep sleep when we have no awareness of anything.

The fourth possibility, corresponding to the transcendental state, occurs when the projector is switched on, but with no film in it. The screen is lit, but there are no images on it: one is awake but there are no objects of experience.

Normally we do not see the screen itself, we only see the images which are being projected on to it. But the screen is still there. Similarly the Self, the screen of the mind, never ceases to exist – without it there could be no experience – but it is usually overshadowed by experience; by the mental images falling upon it.

In the TM technique the intensity of mental activity is reduced until, disappearing completely, only the unchanging screen of pure awareness is left. One is now left in the silent state of pure awareness: wide awake yet completely still.

Infinity and Nothingness

What has effectively happened in transcendental consciousness is that the object of experience and the subject of experience have become the same. The Self has become aware of the Self. In normal experience there is an object of experience, a subject of experience (the Self) and the interaction of the two, which gives rise to the experience. But when consciousness becomes conscious of consciousness, as is happening here, there is no longer any distinction between object and subject and no longer any interaction. Experience as we normally know it ceases. This is why, when the state is first encountered, it often seems to be one of emptiness. The state is nevertheless a very fulfilling one. It is often described as a state of silent joy, and it is this joy which attracts the attention within during the TM technique.

The ancient Indian Upanishads abound with descriptions of the state. Perhaps the clearest is the following taken from the Manduyka Upanishad:[1]

It is not outer awareness, it is not inner awareness, nor a suspension of awareness.

It is not knowing, it is not unknowing, nor is it knowingness itself.

It can neither be seen nor understood,

It cannot be given boundaries.

It is ineffable and beyond thought.

It is indefinable.

It is the end of all activity, silent and unchanging, the supreme good, one without a second.

It is known only through becoming it.

In the West particularly lucid descriptions are to be found in the writings of Plotinus, an Egyptian philosopher living in the third century AD:[2]

In this seeing we neither distinguish nor are there two . . . Only in separation is there duality. This is why the vision baffles telling; for how can a man bring back tidings of the Supreme as detached when he has seen it as one with himself . . . Beholder was one with behold . . . he is become the unity, having no diversity either in relation to himself or anything else . . . reason is in abeyance and intellection, and even the very self, caught away . . . in perfect stillness, all the being calmed . . . there is a communion with the self restored to its purity.

In the present century we find Krishnamurti saying:[3]

> There is a transcendent spontaneity of life, a creative reality which reveals itself as immanent only when the perceiver's mind is in a state of alert passivity . . .
>
> In the ordinary state we have observer and the observed, we have duality – and where there's duality there's conflict. In the transcendental state the observer and the observed become one. There is no longer duality, there's bliss. The thinker and the thought are one.

Some of the finest descriptions of the state are to be found in the great poets. Wordsworth referred to it as 'a happy stillness of the mind . . . a wise passiveness'. In his famous poem *Tintern Abbey* he describes a clear state of transcendental consciousness:

> – that serene and blessed mood,
> In which the affections gently lead us on,
> Until, the breath of this corporeal frame,
> And even the motion of our human blood,
> Almost suspended, we are laid asleep
> In body, and become a living soul.

And Tennyson employing a meditation practice similar to the TM technique reached a state sounding very much like transcendental consciousness as this extract from *The Ancient Sage* indicates:

> More than once when I
> Sat all alone, revolving in myself
> The word that is the symbol of myself,
> The moral limit of the Self was loosed,
> And passed into the nameless, as a cloud
> Melts into heaven.

The Peace which Passeth All Understanding

Most of us tend to associate consciousness so intimately with an object of consciousness that the idea of consciousness without an object seems self-contradictory. One might expect that if all mental activity had ceased then consciousness would also cease. But that would merely amount to a state of deep sleep or coma. Thousands of people the world over have testified that in the transcendental state one is very much awake and alert. Far from being a state of sleep they acclaim it to be one of true wakefulness alongside which our everyday waking state pales to one of semi-sleep. So how are we to conceive of a state in which there is nothing to be conscious of and yet consciousness itself remains?

The answer is probably that we cannot. In trying to understand any new phenomena we naturally try to relate it to what has already been experienced and understood. But when the new material lies beyond the range of our previous experiences this process is not so fruitful. To try to conceive of transcendental consciousness is like a congenitally blind man trying to imagine what colour is. However painstakingly we may describe our visual experiences he will only be able to comprehend them in terms of his previous experiences – tone, taste, touch, etc. It is only when we find a way of giving him the actual *experience* of seeing that he is able to fully appreciate our descriptions and know what 'colour' really means. Similarly, in attempting to understand transcendental consciousness we inevitably try to make it fit with those aspects of thinking with which we are already familiar, i.e. we form concepts of the state. But the state of transcendental consciousness, being beyond all mental activity, is, quite literally, beyond conception.

One sometimes hears it said that the aim of meditation is successively to eliminate all thoughts until one is left 'thinking of nothing'. But thinking of nothing is unfortunately still thinking of something and cannot therefore be a state of transcendental consciousness. Thinking about the state can only create an image of the state, not the experience itself, and such practices are no more than idol worship of a subtle kind.

In transcendental consciousness one quite literally 'hasn't the faintest idea' – either of the state itself or of anything else. If you *think* that you are in the state then you can be pretty sure that you are not, for it lies beyond thought. Being beyond the active mind the state lies beyond any possibility of being perceived by the senses, conceived of by the mind, understood by the intellect, or felt by the emotions. The sixteenth-century Spanish writer, St John of the Cross, describing this feature (or perhaps we should say non-feature) of the state, said:[4]

We receive this mystical knowledge . . . in none of the kinds of images, in none of the sensible representations which our mind makes use of in other circumstances. Accordingly in this knowledge, since the senses and imagination are not employed, we get neither form nor impression, nor can we give any account or furnish any likeness, although the mysterious and sweet tasting wisdom comes here so directly to the innermost parts of the soul.

Because it has none of the usual qualities of thought, any attempt to describe the state becomes a contradiction. To say anything at all about the attributeless is to give it some attribute – even to say that it is attributeless is to give it the attribute of attributelessness. Perhaps we should, like the Buddha, remain silent on the subject, but this is of little help to most people. Yet to take the opposite course and say that it has the particular quality 'A', immediately demands the qualifications that it is also 'not-A'. Conversely, to deny that it has the quality 'A' immediately demands the qualification 'nor is it not-A'. Dionysius, living around the fifth century AD, wrote that: 'nor can any affirmation or negation apply to it'. But equally, enjoying the paradox, we could say that the opposite is also true and that all affirmations and negations may apply to it.

Some philosophers, finding the notion of pure consciousness to be so self-contradictory, have rejected any possibility of its existence. A few have even gone so far as to remark that it is merely that state which inclines one to speak rubbish. But the fact that descriptions of the state appear to be paradoxical does not necessarily invalidate the state: it may merely reflect the weakness of our language and the limitations of a solely rational approach to the study of consciousness. It is not therefore surprising that those who depend almost entirely on logical arguments and the structure of their own language in their quest for truth should find descriptions of pure consciousness a little hard to accept. But to deny its existence is like a blind man denying the possibility of light – to other blind people his arguments may seem plausible and even laudable, but to the person who can see they are empty and pathetic.

The Pure Self

The state of transcendental consciousness has been referred to as the true Self. This does not mean to imply that all other concepts of the self are necessarily wrong. Many of the philosophical, psychological and sociological concepts of personal identity may be quite valid personal attributes. But the pure Self is quite separate from all these concepts and images.

When psychologists talk of the self or ego they may be referring to any one of a number of different concepts. These include the self image we put on to other people, the self we see ourselves as, the self we would like to be seen as, our personalities, unconscious characteristics of our thinking, our sense of unity as an individual person, and many others. But these are all concerned with particular attributes of the individual and are not therefore the same as the pure attributeless Self.

The same could be said of sociological conceptions of the self. For example, the view that our conception of self is conditioned by our social environment may well be true, but here one is talking of a different self from the pure Self which underlies *all* experience, including the conditioned self.

We all have various *ideas* of what we are and how we see ourselves. We talk of ourselves referring to 'my body', 'my mind', 'my experiences', 'my personality', 'my ego', etc. But these are all objects of experience, things that I think I am: they are not the pure Self, the 'I' that thinks and is the subject of all experience.

The pure Self might be thought of as the beam of consciousness shining out from within, and, by taking form, giving rise to everything we are aware of. To look for the pure Self is like taking a torch to look for the source of light, all that we find are a variety of objects giving form to the light. This is why the philosopher Hume's search for his self was bound to failure from the start. In a now famous passage he wrote:[5]

> I always stumble on some particular perception or other, of
> heat or cold, light or shade, love or hatred, pain or pleasure.
> I never can catch *myself* at any time without a perception,
> and can never observe anything but the perception.

But it would be very wrong to conclude that there was no such thing as the Self. The very fact that we are conscious shows that a subject of consciousness exists just as the very fact that light is reflected from other objects allowing us to see, shows that somewhere there is a source of light.

The only way to know the pure Self is by systematically reducing the impact of sensory experience until only the Self remains. This is what happens in transcendental consciousness. In this state there is no longer any experience of 'I am this' or 'I am that'. There is not even the *experience* of 'I am'. It is simply a state of is-ness or pure Being. It is a field which lies beyond individual consciousness and for precisely this reason there is an absence of individuality. If there is any feeling of identity it is one of universality; an at-one-ness with the whole of creation. The boundaries which usually serve to distinguish one self from another having dissolved, there is no longer any effective means of distinction. One begins to experience that, at the most fundamental level, 'we are all one and the same', and that the pure Self is a Universal Self which, shining through different nervous systems, takes on the form of an individual consciousness and individual self. In the words of the psychologist Carl Rogers: 'the deeper that we go into ourselves as particular and unique, seeking for our own individual identity, the more that we find the whole human species.'[6]

The Absolute

Along with most Eastern traditions and many Western ones, Maharishi holds that there is an absolute basis not only to all conscious minds but to everything in existence. He refers to this absolute as the field of pure creative intelligence. In Chapter 3 we saw how every thought possesses the qualities of creativity and intelligence and how the source of thought may be thought of as a field of pure creative intelligence. What he is now saying is that the same could be said of everything that exists.

Nothing we experience is permanent but is subject to ceaseless change. Old forms disintegrate and new patterns and structures are created. This ceaseless activity Maharishi refers to as the principle of creativity. But the changes do not occur at random: objects move subject to well-defined mathematical laws; organisms direct their chemical changes so as to preserve a certain orderliness; and the whole of human learning can be seen as man's attempt to find order beneath continual change. This underlying orderliness is what Maharishi refers to as the principle of intelligence. If everything in the relative world displays these principles of creativity and intelligence then the absolute of which they are formed must itself be a field of pure creative intelligence.

Maharishi therefore sees two aspects to existence; there is the unmanifest field of pure creative intelligence, the absolute aspect; and there are all the various manifestations which we experience, the relative aspects. The absolute aspect can never be detected by the senses or by science. Both are concerned with detecting events, i.e. changes in the world, and the absolute, by definition, is unchanging. Its existence cannot therefore be proved or disproved in the same way that events in the relative world can. All that we can detect and measure are the forms which it takes. In much the same way we can never see pure light. Whenever we see light we see particular colours and particular boundaries – the various forms which light takes – but pure light without colour or form remains essentially unknowable.

The idea that everything we observe is relative, that there is no absolute which can be defined or measured, is also found in Einstein's Special Theory of Relativity. This proposes that space and time are not absolute. What I perceive as space and time will only be the same as what you perceive as space and time if we happen to be travelling together at the same velocity. There is no absolute space or absolute time, only a space-time continuum which, when observed, manifests as a particular perception of relative space and relative time. Similarly Einstein's famous equation, $E = mc^2$, shows that matter and energy are, like space and time, interchangeable and not absolute entities.

The idea of an underlying oneness to all creation can also be seen from a consideration of the fine structure of matter. As one passes from the everyday perception of an object through the microscopic levels of molecules and on to the level of sub-atomic particles there is a tendency away from diversity towards oneness. The infinite variety of objects that we perceive around us is constructed out of various combinations of several million different molecules. These in turn are formed by specific combinations of a hundred different atoms, which are themselves particular combinations of just a few sub-atomic particles. We are moving away from diversity towards sameness.

As we inquire further into the nature of these sub-atomic particles even the concept of particle begins to disappear. Discrete solid objects dissolve into infinite waves extending throughout space-time and representing only tendencies to exist rather than individual existences. The idea of an isolated particle no longer has any meaning. At this level all that exists is a relationship between the observer and his observation; the distinction between

'I' and the World fades. In short, the further we continue to divide and separate the physical world the more we find ourselves being thrown back to the idea of Oneness and inseparability.

It is sometimes assumed, particularly in certain Indian philosophies, that if everything in creation is ultimately the same then the complex diversity which we observe around us is somehow unreal and illusory. But it is not an either-or situation. It is not that, the absolute being real, the relative world of phenomena must be unreal: both are very real. On one level of reality this book is a book; on another level it is also an organized mass of wood fibre; it is also a vast collection of molecules; and from another point of view it is just pure creative intelligence. None of these different views destroys the validity of any other view, they are all different perspectives of reality and are all just as real as each other.

Although it is not possible to experience the absolute in the same way that everything else is experienced, i.e. as a sensory experience, it is possible to know it through personal participation with it. This is what is achieved during the TM technique as the boundaries of awareness dissolve, and one comes to experience pure Being beyond its manifold expressions. Thus the pure Self experienced in meditation as well as being a Universal Self, the basis of all minds, is also the basis of all creation. This is the central theme of the Upanishads:[7]

> What is within us is also without.
> What is without us is also within.

And Plotinus, ever lucid and concise, wrote:[8]

> Each being contains in itself the whole intelligible world. Therefore All is everywhere. Each is there All and All is each. Man as he now is has ceased to be the All. But when he ceases to be an individual, he raises himself again and penetrates the whole world.

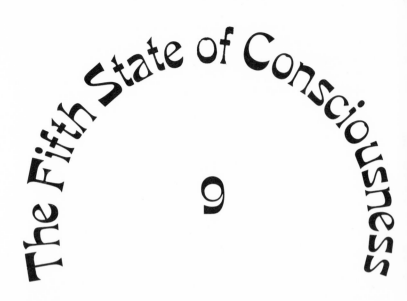

The Fifth State of Consciousness

9

Before enlightenment chop wood and carry water;
After enlightenment chop wood and carry water.

Zen aphorism

By definition the fourth state of consciousness, transcendental consciousness, is the deepest state which can be reached during the TM technique and in this respect it could be said to be the goal of the technique itself. It is not, however, the sole or final aim of the practice. There are several 'higher' states of consciousness which develop as a result of regular contact with transcendental consciousness.

I shall use the word 'higher' to refer to states of consciousness in which the normal perceptions of the waking, dreaming and deep sleep states of consciousness have been added to in some way or another. The unmodified waking, dreaming and deep sleep states I shall call the 'ordinary' states of consciousness. Transcendental consciousness, being a state of pure consciousness, is therefore neither an ordinary nor a higher state of consciousness. It is in a unique category of its own.

The first of the higher states of consciousness, the fifth state of consciousness, is defined as that state in which transcendental consciousness is maintained along with each of the three ordinary states of consciousness. This state is quite distinct from the four states we have previously encountered.

The most important thing to notice about it is that pure consciousness is now maintained not just in the deepest states of meditation but twenty-four hours a day, even in the deepest sleep. This does not mean that there is any additional mental activity taking place – waking, dreaming and deep sleep continue just as before – but along with each of the three ordinary states there is also the awareness of the unchanging field of pure consciousness deep within.

Before the dawn of the fifth state of consciousness the finer levels of thinking and the source of thought itself could only be experienced by withdrawing from activity. One had to temporarily retire from the world of change. But in the fifth state the unchanging basis of the mind can be experienced along with the changing surface levels of thought. This corresponds to the full expansion of the conscious mind which we looked at in Chapter 7. Thinking now embraces all strata of mental activity and on this account Maharishi calls it *cosmic* consciousness.

The importance of this fifth state of consciousness lies in the fact that a person now retains an awareness of the true Self throughout all activity and I shall consider the consequences of this in the next chapter; here I shall be concerned with how the state develops.

The Development of Cosmic Consciousness

Maharishi has always maintained that to every state of consciousness there is a corresponding state of physical activity in the body and that it is only by producing a profound change in physiology and brain functioning that one can ever produce a profound and lasting change in consciousness. If there is no corresponding change from the physical side then any perceived mental change will only be a mood superimposed on the waking state. Thus there are two complementary ways in which one may consider the development of the fifth state of consciousness.

One can look at it either from a consideration of the changes occurring within the body (in terms of the effects of releasing stress), or one may consider the parallel changes which are taking place in the mind (the process of 'infusion' of pure consciousness into the awareness).

The Fifth State of Consciousness

1. As the Purification of the Nervous System

It will be recalled that one of the premises of Maharishi's teaching is that we are usually only conscious of the surface levels of mental activity. What prevents us from being aware of the subtler levels of thinking, and of the field of pure consciousness itself, is the existence of stress in the nervous system. The fifth state of consciousness is only reached when all accumulated stress has been dissolved.

Since it is a permanent state of consciousness the individual must be *permanently* free from stress. It is one thing temporarily to free the nervous system from the effects of stress and so have a passing 'flash' of the fifth state. It is quite another thing to completely rid the nervous system of stress so that no more is ever accumulated.

One might think that the quickest way to develop the state would be to sit down and practise the TM technique continually, day in and day out, until all the stresses had been dissolved. Even though you might temporarily relieve the body of all accumulated stresses by continual meditation, the body would still be susceptible to further experiential overloads and the first burden that the senses encountered would result in stress being accumulated once again. The pure awareness would begin to fade and you would soon find yourself returning to the ordinary waking state.

Activity as well as meditation is fundamental to the development of the fifth state of consciousness. Maharishi teaches that after some stress has been dissolved by the TM technique the nervous system, by which he means the whole organism, must be 'exercised' in order that it may adjust to its new style of functioning. Activity allows the body to recover from the impairment the stress produced and to return towards normal. The fifth state comes about when, through the regular alternation of rest and activity, the nervous system has both released all its accumulated tensions and simultaneously developed a resilience to any further stress.

The fact that people in this state of consciousness no longer accumulate stress does not mean that they are in any way less aware – it is very likely that they will be more fully aware: it is simply that a strong experience will not have the same adverse physiological effects on them. Maharishi likens this to the difference between drawing a line on stone and drawing a line on water. The line drawn on stone leaves a permanent scratch on the surface which is only removed with difficulty: the line drawn on water is the same line, but it leaves no permanent trace. In cosmic consciousness an experience is like a line drawn on water: the experience is perceived but the nervous system is no longer 'scratched' by it.

It is important to realize that the state is not one of sensitivity and fragility where the slightest intrusion of stress must be continually guarded against: it is a state of complete composure in the face of all adversity, when nothing can overshadow the experience of pure awareness. When asked for a test of cosmic consciousness, Maharishi once replied: 'The ability to stand in the middle of Manhattan and still maintain the experience of the Self'.

2. As the Infusion of Pure Consciousness into the Surface Mind

On returning from the deeper levels of thought to the surface levels one usually finds that some of the qualities of the transcendental state have, so to speak, been drawn up into the conscious mind. One experiences this as a sense of wholeness, fullness and stability: an awareness of silence and peace deep within. This Maharishi refers to as the infusion of pure consciousness, or pure Being, into the conscious mind.

At first one may find that these qualities are only present when one is still fairly deep in meditation and that as one returns to the surface they fade away. Later one may find that they are there immediately after meditation but that they quickly fade again as soon as one engages in any sort of activity. It might be concluded that activity should be avoided, or that if one did act then one should try to remain detached from it in order to preserve the state of pure consciousness, as long as possible. But this is not the case. Maharishi repeatedly emphasizes that it is only by allowing the experience of pure awareness to fade away through activity that the nervous system can be 'cultured' to a state where it can continue to maintain pure awareness in all activity.

He frequently likens this process of infusion to the dyeing of cloth using the old vegetable dyes common in rural India. When the cloth is dyed, two processes are necessary. First the cloth is dipped into the dye becoming strongly coloured. But then, since the dyes are not fast, one has to leave it in the sun to fade. After fading it must be again dipped in the dye and again left to fade.

The process is repeated, dipping and fading, dipping and fading, each time the colour becoming a little stronger, until eventually the cloth is so fully dyed that it now no longer fades, even when left in the brightest of suns.

The alternation of rest and activity which occurs with the TM technique can be seen to be a similar process: during the technique the awareness is 'dipped' into pure consciousness and the mind returns 'dyed' with the qualities of pure consciousness; afterwards these qualities are 'faded' by activity. This process is repeated day by day until ultimately the mind is so permanently 'dyed' with pure consciousness that even the strongest experience will not overshadow it.

It is important to note that, having dipped the cloth in the dye, nothing more is to be gained by leaving it there. Likewise, having 'dipped' the attention in pure consciousness nothing more is to be gained by staying within. It is the regular alternation of dipping and fading that is important rather than the dipping itself.

We could bring these two descriptions of the growth of cosmic consciousness together by likening the human nervous system to a crystal. A crystal sparkles and shines as if it were a source of light itself, and the quality of the sparkle depends very much on the purity of the crystal. If there are irregularities and disorders in its structure then it becomes dull and ceases to sparkle so brilliantly. Similarly the human being can shine and sparkle with life from within but if there are irregularities, that is stresses, in the system then we too become dull. We cease to reflect pure consciousness in its fullest values.

The TM program might therefore be considered as a polishing of the 'reflector of consciousness' (the nervous system) so that pure consciousness begins to shine out brighter from within. When ultimately all the stresses have been dissolved then pure consciousness shines out in its full brilliance.

On the Importance of Being Active

By 'activity' Maharishi means any process, physical or mental, in which the attention is directed out towards the senses rather than in towards finer levels of thinking. In effect this means anything other than the TM technique. So when he says that the way to progress is to 'meditate and act' he is emphasizing the value of getting on with things rather than wallowing in post-meditative bliss. He does not mean that after practising the TM technique you should sprint round the block or do a hundred press-ups; but that you should engage yourself wholeheartedly in your normal daily activities. In this respect, an Oxford don philosophizing in his leather armchair is as much engaged in activity as a labourer digging the road. What is important is that whatever you are doing you should be thoroughly involved in it and not try to maintain a sense of detachment. Only in this way will you begin to infuse the effects of meditation into your everyday life.

There is no need to modify one's daily life in order to get the most out of the TM program. In fact, deliberately holding on to the peaceful feeling that persists after meditation only retards the development of cosmic consciousness. Whatever it is one is trying to hold on to, being an idea or image in the mind, could not itself be pure consciousness. It is the effects of contact with pure consciousness that are experienced on the surface of the mind; pure consciousness itself remains silent and unchanging.

People who try to remain detached from activity in an attempt to maintain pure awareness lose out in all ways. Firstly, they only maintain an idea or image of the Self. Secondly, the real process of infusion is hindered. And thirdly, their half-hearted activity is less effective than that of a fully committed man. Rather than progressing they stagnate.

Not only is activity vital for the development of higher states of consciousness, it continues to remain an important characteristic of life when the higher state has been reached – a fact well exemplified in the lives of many enlightened men, including Maharishi's. As the Zen aphorism puts it: 'Before enlightenment, chop wood and carry water; After enlightenment, chop wood and carry water.'

The Gentle Dawn

One important aspect of the growth to the fifth state of con-sciousness is its naturalness and gentleness. One rarely awakes to find oneself suddenly enlightened. One gradually begins to maintain more and more of pure awareness for longer and longer periods of time until ultimately it is there as an all-time, per-manent reality. In this respect the gentle rise to cosmic con-sciousness is like the gentle change from night to day.

As the dawn breaks the intensity of the light increases ten-millionfold, but the change is so smooth and gradual that we hardly notice it. We do not usually observe the light itself increasing: all we notice is that gradually our vision is becoming clearer. Similarly, with the dawning of cosmic consciousness, the gradual brightening of awareness is not itself noticed. If people notice anything it is that their perception is now clearer, their action more effective and the whole of life richer and more enjoyable than it was before.

A smooth continual change is always much harder to notice than an abrupt or intermittent change, and many TM practitioners do not notice the change in themselves although their friends who only see them intermittently often see it very clearly.

It is important that the change is accomplished in such a gentle and unobtrusive manner. Just as a sudden increase in light may be temporarily blinding, so a sudden change from the 'darkness' of the ordinary waking state to the 'full light' of cosmic consciousness might be too overwhelming. By allowing this new level of consciousness to grow in a very natural manner it is integrated harmoniously into one's life.

On first hearing of the idea of cosmic consciousness people frequently try to interpret it in terms of additional experiences at the conscious level of thinking. They think they will start to have wonderful visions or some other extraordinary experiences. But cosmic consciousness is just becoming more truly oneself; becoming the Self. As Anthony Campbell remarks in his book *The Seven States of Consciousness,* rather than undergoing an extraordinary experience one feels as if one is becoming more and more normal.

Maharishi takes this idea of normality a stage further. For him the fifth state of consciousness is the 'normal' state of consciousness. The fact that most people are living in a state of stress and mental dullness does not mean that such states are either natural or necessary. As far as Maharishi is concerned they are 'sub-normal' states. Given the chance the body will throw off stress and purify itself – what Maharishi refers to as the normalization of the nervous system. It is in this respect that he sees the stress-free state as the normal and natural state of life. His aim is to make the fifth state of consciousness the 'normal' state of consciousness both in his sense of the word normal *and* in its everyday sense.

Self-Realization

10

Whoever dieth before his death, getteth relieved of a world of sorrows.

Mohammed

In the fifth state of consciousness the pure Self has become a permanent feature of the awareness and for this reason the state is often known as one of permanent Self-realization. An awareness of the pure Self does not, however, involve any loss of individual self or ego. These continue to function very much as before but added to these individual attributes is a silent awareness of the attributeless Self, the pure 'I', underlying them. This results in a profound and permanent change in personal identity and it is this which makes cosmic consciousness so significant and valuable.

Before Self-realization a person derives his sense of identity from his interaction with the world around. Reduced to its simplest level this interaction is a cycle of action, impression and desire. Every sensory experience leaves some impression in the brain. On the basis of this impression and other past impressions (i.e. memories) we make decisions. This gives rise to various desires and we try to fulfil, and thereby reduce, these desires through appropriate action. The action changes the environment producing new sensory experiences, these in turn giving rise to further desires and action. So the cycle continues.

In cybernetic terms it is a simple feedback loop through which we are able continually to adjust to and interact with our environment.

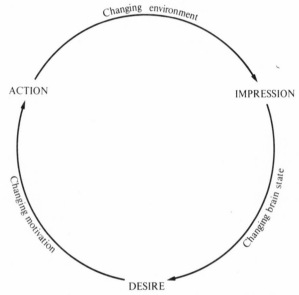

Figure 10 *The cycle of action–impression–desire.*

The continuance of the cycle also provides the organism with a biological identity. It comes to know itself as a semi-autonomous creature interacting with its environment and the sense of individuality which this provides ensures that the organism will strive to stay alive.

Unfortunately the person who is unaware of the pure Self must also rely upon this biological function for a sense of psychological identity and personal existence. Thus we often find ourselves acting not out of some biological need but out of a psychological need – the need to reinforce our sense of personal identity. Indeed, without such continual feedback most of us would die psychologically (literally cease to be) as surely as we would die physically if deprived of food or oxygen.

When changes in the outside world threaten this derived sense of identity we are forced to reaffirm our selves. This may happen in a number of ways. We may filter experience so as only to see what we want to see, we may suppress memories of experiences which threaten our identity or we may find ourselves desiring and acting only for the good of our self-image. How often have we found ourselves defending a point of view not because we really believe it but purely to defend our identity with that point of view? Or when criticized in some way, we may feel psychologically 'hurt'. Ideally we should tend to the cause of the criticism but more often the injured ego demands that it be healed and made to feel strong again. We may do this by retaliating with another criticism, by making attempts to justify ourselves and so save our sense of identity, or, possibly, by pretending to ourselves that we have not even heard it. The net result is that a great deal of psychological and physical energy is wasted on activities which are not only unnecessary and inappropriate, but often damaging to ourselves and our environment.

Now the search for a stable identity is not itself wrong. It is in fact a very basic drive. Indeed, when we recall that the pure Self is experienced as bliss we can see that the search for a stable identity is but another manifestation of the same drive which earlier we saw as the search for greater satisfaction. When there is no awareness of the true Self within, one must seek to derive a permanent and stable identity from the outer world – a world where only change exists – and such a derived identity, being continually at the mercy of events, must be continually reaffirmed. But as a person grows towards cosmic consciousness and gains a greater awareness of the Self the amount of energy and effort which he spends on maintaining his derived sense of identity decreases. When he reaches cosmic consciousness he knows the Self to be a permanent feature of life. From this platform of utter stability he remains unshaken by changes in the outer world. He no longer needs to act and experience in order to derive and maintain a sense of identity. Action now springs not from the demands of the ego but from the demands of the whole situation. This, as we shall see in Chapter 15, is the beginning of true altruism.

Freedom from Bondage

Maharishi continually emphasizes that the enlightened man gains *freedom from bondage* to the cycle of action–impression–desire: he does not have to break or destroy the cycle itself. The Self-realized person still acts and the fruits of his actions still affect his body and his mind, but since his identity is now derived from the inner Self changes in the outer world are no longer threatening. But as a physical organism he is still as subject to the law of physics as anyone or anything else.

Confusion frequently arises over this distinction and it is closely bound up with the confusion over free-will and determinism.

Looking at the universe from a physical point of view it appears that everything that happens is controlled by the laws of physics and just has to happen that way, i.e. everything is completely predetermined. Yet looking at the world from a subjective point of view, we often experience that we choose the way we will act, i.e. we have free-will. It is commonly thought that these two statements are irreconcilable and it is concluded that the experience of free-will may be only an illusion, that physics may not after all be completely deterministic, or that the mind is somehow able to contravene the laws of physics.

There are, however, other possibilities besides this absolutist either-or approach. It may well be that the deterministic and the libertarian interpretations of reality are just two different views of reality which arise from taking different stands with respect to the self. The deterministic view treats the self as an object, the recipient of actions, whereas the libertarian point of view treats the self as a subject, the agent of actions. These two views represent two very fundamental polarities. It is not therefore surprising that the conclusions which they engender are also diametrically opposite.

A similar situation is encountered in quantum physics. It is found that under certain conditions light behaves as waves and under other conditions as particles. At first this contradictory behaviour was very confusing. Niels Bohr, however, suggested that it should be seen in terms of complementarity, and that whether a phenomenon is interpreted as a wave or as a particle depends ultimately upon the way in which the phenomena is observed. Similarly, whether the universe appears to be completely predetermined or open to modification by human free-will depends upon the way in which one observes the situation. From the outside, human beings are as predetermined as the rest of the universe: from the inside, we experience free-will.

The question as to which is right or as to how the two can be reconciled arises from the attempt to transfer terms from one frame of reference to the other. The concept of free-will refers to a subjective experience: it cannot be applied to the physical world where it is meaningless. Similarly, determinism is a concept which arises from an understanding of the physical world and has no relevance to subjective experience. It is not a question of which view is right and which is wrong: both are right relative to the frame of reference from which they arose.

Before the state of Self-realization is gained only the bounded individual self is known and this one self is forced to play two contradictory roles. Firstly, it has to maintain a sense of individuality and personal freedom; yet secondly this same self, being derived from the external world, must also suffer the ups and downs of that world, i.e. it is also deterministic. One is forced to try and fit two mutually contradictory perspectives of the world into one frame of reference. This inevitably results in confusion and paradox. But for the self-realized man there is no conflict. The individual self is still as bound as ever – all his actions, including his thoughts, are still subject to deterministic laws: but the pure Self is completely free. In this way the paradox has been resolved – or rather dissolved.

Thus the enlightened person does not gain freedom from the deterministic cycle of action, impression and desire, but freedom from psychological bondage to this cycle. 'It is not,' writes Maharishi,[1] 'the action or its fruits which bind a man; rather it is the inability to maintain freedom which becomes a means of bondage.' Unfortunately this point is too often missed. It is frequently held that in order to escape from bondage to the cycle the cycle itself must be stopped or broken in some way, and various techniques have grown up with the intention of doing just this.

When action has been seen to be at fault, people have tried to modify or reduce their activity in the hope that they would thereby reduce their bondage to the world. Others, believing experience to be at fault, have advocated sensory control and withdrawal in order that further desires may not be stimulated – that one may not be led into temptation. And others, thinking that desires were the cause of bondage and suffering have sought to eliminate all desires. But all these approaches deliberately disrupt the natural biological feedback processes and can have a disastrous effect on daily life. Moreover it is doubtful whether, by themselves, such practices could ever lead to true Self-realization, which, by definition, is the ability to live the pure Self *along with* the natural processes of action, experience and desire.

The Still Point of a Turning World

Self-realization does not entail awareness of the Self at the expense of self. The action–impression–desire cycle continues and with it the sense of individual identity. All that goes to make up a unique individual is still there; the enlightened person retains his character, personality, memories, etc. The path to Self-realization is not therefore one of self-abnegation, self-subordination or self-elimination; it is one of expansion of awareness to include the pure Self along with the individual self.

One might liken the Self to the hub of the revolving wheel of life. Individual ego, memories, images, experiences, desires, thoughts, etc., continually revolve around the pure Self. The Self, being at the center, never changes. In Self-realization the wheel has not stopped, it continues to revolve much as before, but one has now also become aware of the center of the wheel, and one draws one's identity not from the spinning rim of the wheel but from its still center.

In the TM program the state of Self-realization is brought about by allowing the attention repeatedly to retire from the cycle of action–impression–desire into transcendental consciousness. No attempt is made to break the cycle, but, by allowing the mind to settle down, activity, experience and desire all spontaneously decrease. The cycle temporarily dies away. In transcendental consciousness only the Self remains. Then through activity the awareness of the pure Self is integrated into daily life.

Returning to cinema screen analogy of Chapter 8 we could say that now both the screen and the film are known separately. But knowing the screen for what it really is in no way destroys the film. What maintains the individual identity of the film is the coherence and continuity of its images and this is not lost when the screen is discovered. In the waking state one identifies with the continuity of experience, i.e. the images falling upon the screen of the mind, whereas in the fifth state of consciousness one knows oneself to be pure consciousness: the screen itself. The continuity of experience does not cease; it continues as before. But it is no longer mistaken for the screen, the pure Self.

When people try to understand this new state of consciousness they inevitably do so in terms of previously encountered states and frequently conclude that it must involve some kind of separation between the mind and body, or between the ego and the mind. But this is not the case. Self-realization is a clear separation between the silent attributeless Self and *all* activity, mental and physical; a separation between the Self on the one hand and the body, senses, mind, intellect, emotions, *and* ego on the other.

Non-Attachment

Because the sense of identity is no longer derived from nor conditioned by the ego, mind, senses or body, the state of Self-realization is often referred to as one of non-attachment. Unfortunately the real meaning of non-attachment has been frequently misunderstood, resulting in a rejection of all material possessions and anything else which gave one pleasure, with the intention that the individual would no longer be 'attached' to the outside world. But this only creates an image or mood of non-attachment and eventually leads to the most bizarre forms of hypocrisy. *Non-attachment has nothing to do with the avoidance of action or pleasure. It is the ability to act and enjoy in freedom without being bound to the process for a sense of identity.* As it says so clearly in the Bhagavad Gita:

> Not by refraining from action does a man achieve freedom
>   from action;
> Nor by mere renunciation does he attain supreme perfection.
> Not even for a moment can a man be without action;
> For all are helplessly driven to action by the forces born of
>   Nature.
> He who withdraws himself from actions, but ponders on
>   their pleasures in his heart,
> He is deceiving himself, and can only be called a hypocrite.
>   (III: 4-6)

Attachment arises when the sense of identity is drawn from experience and action. If a man partly draws his sense of identity from his car, for example, then he is said to be attached to it, for if his car were to go, his identity would suffer. Non-attachment occurs when the identity is drawn from the pure Self. This does not mean that the Self-realized man would cease to care about the outer world or become insensible to its ups and downs: but, being grounded in the Self, his identity or sense of personal existence is not shaken by changes in the outer world.

It is in this sense that Maharishi talks of the absence of suffering. The Self-realized person can still incur great emotional loss – indeed, his emotions will probably be much richer than before – but being no longer bound to his experience for his sense of identity, *he*, as the unchanging Self, can no longer be shaken by outer change and is, therefore, beyond the very possibility of suffering. Any losses are borne with grace and fortitude without the need to heal an injured ego.

Suffering, concludes Maharishi, is born of a false identification with experience. This does not mean that personal suffering is in any way unreal. For the person whose awareness does not pass beyond the surface levels of existence suffering is very real, and any talk of it not being so is clearly ridiculous. But for the Self-realized person there is the additional reality of a level of life which lies beyond pleasure and pain, and at this level there is no suffering.

Nor will the Self-realized person be insensible to the suffering of others. He is beyond personal suffering, it is true, but from this unshakeable stand he will be more sensitive to the plight of others and better able to help them. As Maharishi remarks:[2]

> A happy man would be able to see the unhappiness of others much more than an unhappy man. An unhappy man is busy suffering himself, he has no time to see the suffering of others. Compassion is not awake in an unhappy, miserable mind. But compassion and kindness are awake in a man who is happy, who is peaceful.

Looking back over history we find that many people in higher states of consciousness devoted their lives to alleviating the suffering of others – indeed, it is one of the commonly accepted characteristics of a saint that he should have given himself 'selflessly' to the benefaction of mankind.

It is sometimes held that, since it is the ego ('the illusory self') which is at the root of suffering, the ego must die. If this means that the false identification with the ego must cease then it is, with a qualification or two, acceptable: but if it means that the individual ego must be destroyed, as some contemporary Buddhists appear to believe, then it is clearly untenable. (I say 'contemporary' Buddhists because it is possible that the original teachings of the Buddha were much closer to those of Maharishi in this respect. Sidney Spencer, for example, argues that there is considerable evidence that the Buddha did teach of an attributeless pure Self very close to that of the Upanishads.[3])

Those who adhere to this latter interpretation teach that all suffering involves 'I': 'I want this', 'I have not got that', etc., and *therefore* the 'I' must go. But this is a denial of the changing Self rather than an affirmation of the changeless Self and the path then becomes one of self-destruction rather than Self-discovery – an approach which can only result in self-deceit. Unless a person first establishes an identity with the pure Self any attempt to rid himself of an illusory identity will only result in the creation of a new sense of identity and the replacement of one illusion by another.

Transcending Desire

When suffering is thought to result from the 'craving of I', then it is taught that in order to eliminate suffering one must first eliminate all desires. Maharishi strongly disagrees with this. It is not, he says, desires themselves which lead to suffering but one's inability to fulfil them. Unfulfilled desires are the cause of suffering and unhappiness.

He teaches that the way to get rid of unfulfilled desires is not to try to banish or subjugate the desires themselves but effectively to fulfil them by achieving the goal of all desires. This is not to say that one must actually fulfil all possible desires – some desires may be beyond any physical possibility of fulfilment while others may conflict with someone else's, making it impossible for everyone to fulfil them all: it is the ultimate goal of all desires rather than the desires themselves which must be fulfilled.

The origin of many desires is the search for a stable identity. When the pure Self has become a permanently established feature of the awareness one has effectively achieved the ultimate goal of these desires and the desires themselves no longer arise. In this way one has satisfied these desires without actually having to fulfil each individually.

Of course not all desires are on the level of ego-maintenance: many of them are a natural part of life. The basic desire for food, for example, is a natural biological one (although it may in the case of compulsive eaters also reflect some abnormal psychological need). It would be very wrong to try to eliminate such necessary drives, and it would be equally wrong to try to eliminate many of man's 'higher' desires for the health and welfare of his community and surroundings. All these natural desires continue to arise in the mind of the Self-realized person, but with one important difference: they do not give rise to craving.

We have seen that every thought starts from the subtlest levels of the mind and rising up to the surface levels of thinking develops into a fully fledged idea. It is only when the impulse has reached the grosser levels of thinking that it takes the form of a desire. Before this it is merely an incentive for action without craving. The person whose attention is confined to the grosser levels of thinking, only appreciates an incentive for action when it has already become a desire; all his actions start from the level of desire. With the coming of Self-realization one experiences the whole range and depth of thinking and is able to appreciate an impulse before it has become strong enough to be a desire. One's thoughts are translated into action without first expressing themselves as desires, and without the craving and suffering which goes with them.[4]

So we can begin to understand why Maharishi says that the enlightened man has no desires as such and why the state is described as one of personal fulfilment. But it is important to realize that the absence of desire is the *result* of gaining fulfilment: to try to eliminate all desires *in order to* rise towards fulfilment is to put the cart before the horse.

Right Action

When Maharishi says that the Self-realized person acts according to the needs of the situation rather than the needs of the ego he is not saying anything specific about his actions. He is not saying that the Self-realized person will do this or that, nor even that he should do this or that: only that his actions will spontaneously be more effective and more suited to the overall situation. But do not misunderstand the nature of this spontaneity. It is not that actions themselves occur any more spontaneously – the actions of the enlightened person are probably no more and no less premeditated than those of his unenlightened fellows – but that whatever actions he decides to undertake will, without any additional deliberation, be more appropriate and more fruitful.

The full effects of any action are unfathomable: they are so far-reaching, both in space and time, that it is beyond the scope of any mind to follow them all through. Even if it were possible to know the full effects of any action this by itself would not dictate whether that action was right or wrong. We must still decide upon the correct ethic by which to evaluate the effects, and in this task reason alone is insufficient.

When it comes down to making a decision we simply act as we feel is best. What Maharishi is saying is that the way we *feel* will spontaneously change as we raise our level of consciousness. We might think of this as the growth of intuition – and in the final analysis it is intuition which is at the basis of all our moral laws however they may subsequently be rationalized and codified. But intuitive feelings of right and wrong are not of course always correct. The degree to which they are right or wrong will depend upon one's clarity of mind. Moreover, one's intuitive responses must still be analysed in the cold light of day and here the synthesis of intuition and reason that develops with the TM program becomes of increasing importance.

Many people find it alarming that Maharishi lays down no moral precepts or codes of behaviour. The TM technique may make a person act more efficiently but what, they ask, is to prevent him from channelling this activity in undesirable directions? Indeed, since the Self-realized person has, in transcending the individual self, transcended the element of personal fear upon which many of our laws depend, what is there to stop him becoming a wanton criminal?

Maharishi's answer is that, in transcending the individual self, the Self-realized person has transcended the very roots of immoral and criminal action, for these stem from the need to maintain a derived sense of identity. His motivations have changed and he simply would not want to engage in such actions. What one begins to notice as one continues with the TM program is that one is refraining from 'wrong' action, not because one has been told it is wrong or because of the fear of punishment, but because it *feels* wrong.

I do not mean to suggest that anyone who practises the TM technique is necessarily more moral than someone who does not – this is clearly not the case: only that the growth of awareness which follows will be accompanied by a spontaneous tendency to act in a more 'life-supporting' manner..The actual moral standing of any particular individual will depend upon where they started from and their speed of personal growth.

The fact that Maharishi never speaks of evil, only of good, could be taken to indicate that he ignores the presence of evil: but this is not the case. He is merely looking at what we would call negative or evil actions from a different point of view. He believes that all actions have the same final goal – union with the fundamental ground of all existence, the Self or Absolute. The most egocentric and selfish actions are only manifestations of the search for the true Self and ultimate fulfilment. In this respect Maharishi sees all action to be for progress and fulfilment. He likens the situation to a man trying to row a flimsy boat across a river. In mid-stream he may encounter a log and be forced, by the frailty of his craft, to turn back temporarily in order to avoid the obstacle, but he is turning back *in order that he may continue towards the other side.* Looking at his manoeuvre out of context, he would seem to be rowing the wrong way, but seen as part of the whole journey it is, under the circumstances, the only possible course of action for him. Someone in a more rugged boat might be able to sail straight ahead ploughing the obstacle aside. Likewise, apparently negative actions can be seen as the attempts of a weak man to cope as best he can with the obstacles which crop up in his journey across the river of life.

But even though the Self-realized person may act more in harmony with his surroundings, Maharishi makes it clear that one can never judge another's state of consciousness by his actions alone. The only criterion of his state of consciousness is an internal one: is Self-awareness established as a permanent reality independent of experience? All that we, as external observers, can know of a Self-realized person is on the level of his words and actions and these are no sure indication of his inner state of consciousness. In the words of the Tao-Te-Ching:[5]

> The ancient masters were subtle, mysterious, profound, responsive,
> The depth of their knowledge is unfathomable.
> Because it is unfathomable,
> All we can do is describe their appearance.

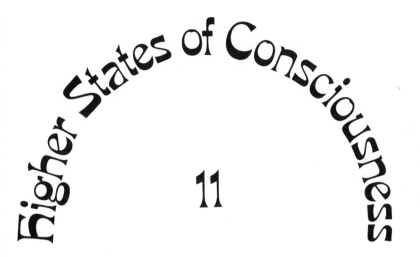

11

As a man is, so he sees.

William Blake

Until now my concern with higher states of consciousness has been limited to the fifth state of consciousness, but Maharishi speaks of several higher states of consciousness beyond this. At first this might seem surprising for does not the fifth state of consciousness involve the full expansion of the mind, an awareness of all levels of mental activity from the gross level right down to the silence of the transcendental state? What more could there be?

By definition the fifth state is that state in which the transcendental state is permanently maintained along with waking, dreaming and deep sleep. There is full inner development along with ordinary daily awareness. But, although the subject of experience, the Self, has become fully known, the perception of objects in the outer world remains much as before. It is this which now begins to develop.

Earlier I suggested that the pure Self, the oneness within, also underlies the whole phenomenal creation. In the normal waking state one only sees the surface levels of life. During the TM technique one experiences the subtler underlying levels of thinking and then, transcending these, gains an awareness of the pure Self within. In the further development beyond the fifth state, one begins to experience the finer underlying levels of objects in the outside world until finally one appreciates the absolute in everything that is perceived, both within and without.

The Sixth State of Consciousness

The first stage of this development is what Maharishi has defined as the sixth state of consciousness. He says that in this state the perception of objects has been refined to the state where one can be aware of the finest levels of relative existence but the perception has not yet been so refined as to take in the absolute value as well.

When he claims that one becomes aware of the finer levels of existence, he does not mean to imply that one actually sees molecules, electrons or anything like that. These only represent the finer levels of an object in terms of its gross physical structure, i.e. as it would appear under a microscope. Maharishi seems to be talking more of the structure of perception than the physical structure of the object, and as far as perception is concerned the finest level of creation is one of pure light.

This is not such a novel idea; similar views are often expressed by both artists and theoretical physicists. What Maharishi is saying is that in the sixth state of consciousness this knowledge becomes a living reality. The perception has developed, or as he puts it, 'been refined', to the point where one is personally aware of this finest level of creation. Everything is seen as if composed of and pervaded by pure light. He refers to this as a state of glorified cosmic consciousness.

There is abundant testimony to such an experience in the writings of poets, mystics and 'visionaries' throughout the ages. Wordsworth would appear to be describing such an experience in his *Ode: Intimations of Immortality from Recollections of Early Childhood*:

> There was a time when meadow, grove and stream,
> The earth, and every common sight,
> To me did seem
> Apparelled in celestial light.

And in 'Il Paradiso' of his *Divine Comedy* Dante wrote of:[1]

> the Eternal Light ... my sight becoming pure was entering more and more through the beam of the lofty light which is itself true ... In its depth I saw that it contained, bound by one volume, that which is scattered in leaves throughout the universe. Substances and accidents and their relations as it were bound together in such a way that what I tell of is a simple light.

And St Augustine noted that:[2]

> It was not the common light which all flesh can see, nor was it greater yet of the same kind, as if the light of day were to grow brighter and brighter and flood all space. It was not like this, but different: altogether different from all such things.

It is in Walt Whitman's words a 'light rare, untellable, lighting the very light – beyond all signs, descriptions and languages'.[3]

As with cosmic consciousness and all higher states of consciousness, it should be made clear that nothing is lost in the development of this state of consciousness. The ordinary gross levels of perception are there just as before, but *added to them* is the perception of the finer levels of creation. A chair is still a chair, but subtler values of the chair, which previously lay beyond perception, now reach awareness.

This heightened perception of the relative world comes from a more intimate appreciation of the absolute. In the fifth state of consciousness the absolute was known only on the subjective level of experience as the pure Self. Now, in the sixth state of consciousness, the awareness of the absolute begins to overflow into one's perception of the objective world. The world begins to appear suffused with the light of the Self, and objects which previously were only appreciated impersonally now begin to take on personal qualities.

The Seventh State of Consciousness

William Blake wrote in *The Marriage of Heaven and Hell*: 'If the doors of perception were cleansed everything will appear to man as it is, infinite.' Such a state of full perception represents the next level of consciousness, what Maharishi sometimes calls the state of 'unity consciousness' or more often just 'Unity', and often refers to as a state of full enlightenment.

In the sixth state of consciousness the doors of perception were only partially cleansed, in this seventh state the perception has become refined to the point where one becomes directly aware of the absolute basis of the outer world. Both the subject of perception and the object of perception are appreciated in their fullest values, as manifestations of the transcendental absolute field of life. Everything, both within and without, is now appreciated in terms of the pure Self.

Meister Eckhart was clearly describing this state when he wrote that:[4]

All that man has here externally in multiplicity is intrinsically One.

Here all blades of grass, wood and stone, all things are One.

This is the deepest depth, and thereby am I completely captivated.

It is important to note that the diversity of creation is not lost in this experience of oneness. 'Here', in the state of Unity, all blades of grass, wood and stone are still perceived as blades of grass, wood and stone, but added to this surface awareness is an appreciation of their underlying unity and common essence. The phenomenal world does not dissolve into some kind of qualityless grey fog. The relative world of infinite diversity continues to exist, but is now experienced as coexisting with its absolute basis.

This coexistence of relative and absolute reflects Maharishi's teaching that the relative world of phenomena is just as real as its absolute basis. I mentioned earlier how the idea has sometimes arisen that if the absolute is real then the relative must be an illusion. In some systems of Indian philosophy this is known as the doctrine of *maya*. But Maharishi insists that it is not the relative world of phenomena that is an illusion – it is very real: the illusion lies in the question of a relationship between the two; in the question 'How does the absolute become all this?' The absolute and the relative are two different perspectives of reality and as such neither can be explained in terms of the other. The relative cannot be accounted for in terms of the absolute, nor can the absolute be understood in terms of the relative.

Imagine you have in your hand a cylindrical block. Looked at from the side it will appear as a square: looked at from the end it will appear as a circle. Fortunately we are able to integrate these partial two-dimensional perspectives of the object in the more comprehensive three-dimensional concept of a cylinder and we find no conflict between the two views. But if we did not have this broader perceptual framework and had to relate everything in a two-dimensional frame of reference we would be faced with an object which appeared sometimes as a square and sometimes as a circle. In this situation the only way to resolve the apparent paradox would be to try and explain one in terms of the other and if this failed declare that one or other must be an illusion. This is the sort of situation that the person in the waking state faces with respect to the absolute and the relative. They are two different perspectives of reality, but since the awareness cannot encompass both simultaneously a paradox arises and it cannot be resolved by simply accommodating one perspective within the other.

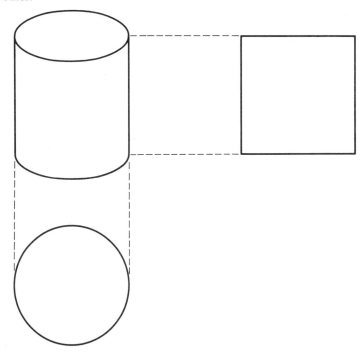

Figure 11 *Two partial and potentially conflicting perspectives of a cylinder.*

It is not that the relative is an illusion, as many Eastern philosophers have tried to say, nor that the absolute is unreal, as many Western thinkers have suggested. Both are real, and the only way truly to resolve the paradox is to expand the awareness to the point where it can encompass both views simultaneously. This happens in Unity when both the absolute and the relative are known fully and independently. In this state there is no problem of how one is to be explained in terms of the other. To the question 'How does the absolute become all this?' the sage simply replies that it is 'Maya' – the relationship is an illusion.

Thus the relative world of phenomena is in no way compromised by the experience of the absolute. On the contrary, it is said to be strengthened and enlivened. 'The differences,' says Maharishi, 'are enjoyed in the full value of infinite harmony.' Appreciating the harmony beneath the diversity one begins to realize that the differences and even the disharmonies are part of a greater pattern.

I remember the idea that even negative influences can be seen to be in harmony being brought out very clearly by an enlightened yogi who lived in the hills above Maharishi's academy at Rishikesh. He was explaining that the Self could be likened to the sun: just as the sun illuminates everything and we see everything in terms of its light, so everything we experience is illuminated by the Self and the enlightened person perceives everything in terms of the Self. Somebody asked if disharmonious or negative influences could obscure the experience of Unity in the same way that clouds obscure the light of the sun. The yogi simply replied: 'Even the clouds are illuminated by the sun!'

But it is important to realize that the state of Unity is not a mere understanding that 'all is One': it is a state of consciousness in which a person experiences his essential unity with the rest of the world. A mere intellectual understanding of this fact cannot by itself give the immediate knowledge which comes from personal experience. Although many philosophers have at various times dwelt upon the idea of an underlying unity one would not guess from reading their analyses and arguments that the actual experience of the state was a most enjoyable and fulfilling one. Indeed, some have even suggested that it would be an unpleasant experience. Yet, those who have personally experienced the state have made very clear that it is a state of peace and fulfilment. Maharishi himself writes:[5]

Every perception, the sound of every word, the touch of every little particle and the smell of whatever may be, brings a tidal wave from the ocean of eternal bliss. Every rising thought, word or action is a rising of the tide of bliss.

In every static or dynamic state of existence the divine glory of the unmanifested is found dancing in the manifested field of life. The absolute dances in the field of the relative. Eternity pervades every moment of transitory existence.

State of consciousness	Awareness of self		Awareness of other objects		
	Individual self	Pure Self	Relative level		Absolute level
			Gross	Subtle	
Deep sleep	—	—	—	—	—
Dreaming	?	—	?	—	—
Waking	✓	—	✓	—	—
Transcendental state	—	✓	—	—	—
Fifth state (cosmic consciousness)	✓	✓	✓	—	—
Sixth state	✓	✓	✓	✓	—
Seventh state (unity)	✓	✓	✓	✓	✓

Figure 12 *The seven states of consciousness.*

First, Know Thyself

The growth of awareness which the TM program brings occurs in an orderly fashion. One starts off from the ordinary, everyday waking state in which there is only a partial appreciation of the objects of experience and the subject of experience. Through regular practice of the TM technique one gains contact with transcendental consciousness and through activity stabilizes this awareness, bringing about the fifth state of consciousness. On the basis of this full subjective development one then gains a full awareness of the object of experience. Thus the direction of development is from the inner to the outer. This is very important.

As the mind becomes clearer and the awareness of the Self stronger there is much less chance of . a strong experience overshadowing the Self. When the fifth state is reached then, by definition, the Self is so established that no experience can overshadow it. As one continues from the fifth to the seventh state one encounters experiences which, from all descriptions, are quite remarkable but the Self being fully established ought not to be obscured by them. If on the other hand one were deliberately to encourage these experiences of refined perception without having first stabilized the Self then there is the danger that they would completely obscure any Self-awareness there might be. Such practices would certainly lead to a welter of most remarkable and sensational experiences, but because they tended to overshadow the Self it is questionable whether they would also lead to a state of full enlightenment.

Another important consequence of developing the states in this order is that the whole process is entirely natural and effortless at every step. We saw in Chapter 4 how, having taken the correct start and let go, the TM process takes place quite spontaneously without any control or coercion on the part of the individual. The same principle applies at every stage of development. From the fourth to the fifth state of consciousness the formula is 'meditate and act': practise the TM technique regularly and effortlessly and carry on with the rest of your life as normal. Then, without any restraints or artificial control of mood, one gently and spontaneously rises to cosmic consciousness. The further development from the fifth state through the sixth to the seventh state of consciousness is likewise effortless and spontaneous.

In practice, the development does not occur in such well-defined stages as the above description would imply. One state can begin to develop on the basis of the partial establishment of the states which underlie it, and so one may have some experience of a higher state before the preceding states have become fully stabilized. This also implies that having reached one state of consciousness the next will already be partially developed. Thus the sixth state will appear to dawn more rapidly than the fifth and the seventh more rapidly still. Maharishi sees this phenomenon as an example of a more general principle: the principle that any development or evolution speeds up as it progresses – a theme which I shall return to in the final chapter.

Removing the Mystery from Mysticism

In several instances I have illustrated parallels between

Maharishi's teachings and those of mystics, but this does not make TM in any way mysterious. Mysticism has very little to do with mystery – indeed, the revelation experienced by the mystic could be said to remove much of the mystery from his world. It is true that mystery and mysticism both come from the same greek root *muo*, meaning to close the eyes and lips and become silent, but whereas a 'mystery' is a lack of knowledge generally resulting from the silence of others, 'mysticism' is a fullness of knowledge brought about by personally retiring from the world into a state of inner silence. Any mystery there may be in mysticism is merely the consequence of an imperfect understanding and insufficient experience of these states.

Sidney Spencer in his excellent study of this field[6] has described mysticism as 'an immediate contact with the Transcendant'; the TM experience clearly satisfies this criterion. Other scholars, such as William James, Walter Stace, Rudolph Otto, F. C. Happold, Marguenita Laski, Evelyn Underhill and Aldous Huxley, who have also studied the teachings and writings of mystics in some detail have tried to establish more specific characteristics of the experience. Examining their conclusions one finds half a dozen commonly recurring themes:

    (1) a feeling of at-oneness with the whole of creation;

    (2) a greater and more profound knowledge of the cosmos;

    (3) the feeling that this knowledge is somehow more real than other knowledge;

    (4) an experience of joy and fulfilment;

    (5) a sense of blessedness and contact with the divine;

    (6) an alleged ineffability (an inability to describe the experience in words).

These characteristics are also common to the higher states of consciousness which develop through the TM program, as I have tried to illustrate in this and previous chapters.

Is The TM Program a Religion?

Maharishi is always at great pains to point out that the TM program is not a religion: it is simply a technique of bringing the mind and body to a state of stillness and accruing the benefits which result.

The *Oxford Dictionary* defines a religion as a 'system of faith and belief' or 'recognition of a superhuman controlling power entitled to obedience'. The TM program, however, involves no faith or belief. The effectiveness of the technique does not depend on whether or not you believe it will work, nor does it depend upon the acceptance of any particular doctrines. Many people practise the TM technique quite happily and quite successfully without accepting any of the theory that Maharishi puts forward to explain the process. Similarly with the 'recognition of a superhuman controlling power', TM students are not asked to recognize any such agency. If there is any controlling power in the TM technique it is the life in each and every one of us rather than some external divinity. Any improvement in the quality of action which comes with the TM program is not due to any obedience to moral injunctions, nor is it a reward from a superhuman controller: it is the spontaneous effect of a clearer consciousness. Right action, as we saw in Chapter 10, is the result of enlightenment, not the path to it.

People begin the TM program from all walks of life, from all religious denominations, and from no particular religious denomination. There is no conflict between the TM technique and one's own personal belief system. In fact, many clergy, including nuns and monks, have started the TM technique and are finding the experience enriching to their own religious life.

The question which should be asked is not 'Is TM a religion?', but 'In what ways can religious traditions benefit from the TM program?' The types of experience to which the TM technique leads are of the same kind as appear to be at the core of every major religious practice. Happold writes that mysticism is 'the raw material of all religions' and William James said similarly that 'personal religious experience has its root and center in mystical states of consciousness.'

It could be argued that the religious traditions must have originally contained practical techniques for directly raising the individual's level of consciousness. But they were inevitably distorted over the ages to an unknown extent and most of what remains today is largely on the level of ritual and faith. It is very much as if a major oil shortage had forced private cars to be discarded and their real function to be forgotten. Many books on cars and driving might survive and various sects might be found ardently reading out passages of incomprehensible material to each other, studying the road maps, and ritually manipulating the controls. But, ignorant of the fact that there was an engine under the bonnet which, given the correct fuel, could make all their dreams come true, their only solace would be the hope that the spirit of Henry Ford might look kindly upon them and bless them with 'a journey'. Some, remembering that the car itself was supposed to move, might develop techniques by which to push it physically down the road, and after much strenuous effort a small journey might indeed be completed. But, without knowledge of the all-important fuel any suggestion that so heavy an object could move of its own accord would be treated with scorn, if not as heresy.

The fuel of religion is the practice which, by its simplicity and effectiveness, allows the man-in-the-street to realize the goals spoken of by the teacher. When this is lost all that remains is a dry and often meaningless intellectual understanding. In the search for meaning the teachings become progressively distorted until very little of the original remains. Countless numbers are left straining at misconceptions, fruitlessly trying to understand what is already a misunderstanding, and more often than not they end up doing the opposite of what was originally intended. So, if today we find a vast array of apparently different techniques and doctrines it may not necessarily be because the original practices were very different: it may well be the result of different cultural and political forces distorting the original in different directions. As William Law remarked in the eighteenth century:[7]

There is not one way for the Jew, another for a Christian, and a third for the Heathen, No; God is one, human nature is one, salvation is one and the Way is one.

But, as the Tao-Te-Ching had already warned:[8]

When the Way is lost, there is goodness,
When goodness is lost, there is kindness,
When kindness is lost, there is justice,
When justice is lost, there is ritual,
Now ritual is the husk of faith and loyalty, the beginning of
    confusion.

As far as India is concerned, Maharishi believes that techniques very similar to the TM technique can be found described in the ancient Sanskrit verses of the Vedas. Most contemporary translations of these texts treat them on the level of mythological tales and hymns. But this, he says, is the shallowest level of interpretation: the Vedas can also be understood at much deeper and far richer levels and when properly interpreted they can be seen to contain precise instructions for meditation which are remarkably similar to the TM technique in the present day.

Traditionally the Vedas were always chanted and handed down as an oral tradition. This is because much of their value lies in the actual sounds of the words which compose them. When written down – or, worse still, when translated – the key to their knowledge is lost; the Vedas are interpreted only on the level of their surface meaning and their true significance is missed.

Ancient Sanskrit was a very compact and concise language. In its written form many redundant words were omitted and the actual meaning of a given phrase depended very much on its context. If the Vedas were concerned with the realization of higher states of consciousness, then it is important that every statement be understood within this context. But if the commentator is not himself in a higher state he is lacking the most fundamental clue to their interpretation. He must base his rendering on the 'traditional' view, thus preserving and supporting the current misconceptions. A faithful commentary of these texts can only be undertaken by one who is living at the same level of consciousness as that from which the texts originated. In India such a person is called a 'rishi' meaning 'seer', the title 'Maharishi' meaning 'great seer'. And Maharishi is himself working on a new commentary of the Vedas with the intention of bringing back to the world a wisdom that has been lost for many centuries.

Maharishi believes that since the time of the Vedas this knowledge has been lost and found many times. As far as India is concerned it has recurred principally in the Bhagavad Gita, the teachings of Buddha, and those of Shankara. He goes into this cycle of loss and revival in some depth in his introduction to the Bhagavad Gita and I highly recommend it for anyone interested in this topic.[9]

But I think it would be a mistake to become too involved in what may or may not have happened in the past. What to me is important is that one has, in the TM technique, the possibility of raising one's own state of consciousness, now. Maharishi has alluded to himself as an engineer with the knowledge of how to repair a road that has, with the passage of time, fallen into disrepair and disuse. In this case, what is important is not to study the holes in the old road or wonder who else may have walked down it in ages past, but to travel on down it ourselves.

Some Psychological Perspectives

12

> To the psychologist the religious propensities of man must be at least as interesting as any other of the facts pertaining to his mental constitution.
>
> William James

Psychology had its roots in philosophy and set out, as its name implies, to be the study of the mind. In its eagerness to appear as a natural science rather than a speculative study it adopted the methodology and techniques of physiology and physics. This led to the development of psychophysics (the physics of perception) and to the establishment of the powerful behaviourist approach which maintained that all that could be objectively studied was the observable behaviour of an organism. Powerful as it was, the behaviourist approach had many shortcomings, in particular it failed to take subjective experience into account.

The first major alternative to behaviourism came with Jean Martin Charcot and the study of the unconscious mind. This was taken up by his pupil Sigmund Freud and subsequently by researchers such as Carl Jung, Alfred Adler and Theodore Reik, to form the basis of the various schools of psychotherapy and psychoanalysis. This approach was certainly more concerned with mental experience – or in most cases with what was not actually experienced – but it tended to focus on those who were mentally sick or psychologically deficient in some way or another.

A steadily growing dissatisfaction with both the experimental-behaviourist approach and the psychoanalytic schools led to the emergence of many splinter groups. In the fifties and sixties these began to coalesce into a third force in psychology, known as Humanistic Psychology. This included psychologists such as Carl Rogers, Rollo May, Erich Fromm and writers such as Herbert Marcuse and Norman Brown, but the greatest single figure in the movement was Abraham Maslow.

Maslow turned away from the study of mentally sick people towards the study of the mentally healthy – the healthiest people that he could find. The people he investigated were all composed, stable, integrated members of society. They all displayed a degree of what he called 'self-actualization': 'the actualization of potential, capacities, and talents, as fulfilment of mission, as a fuller knowledge of and acceptance of the person's own intrinsic nature, as an unceasing trend towards unity, integration or synergy within the person'.[1]

Maslow's studies showed that self-actualizers had a clearer perception of reality, were more creative and spontaneous in their daily life, showed an increased acceptance of self, and were centered on problems external to themselves rather than on the task of ego-maintenance. They had a strong sense of identity with humanity as a whole and were consequently capable of deeper personal relationships without having to bother about social status. They also tended to be optimists rather than pessimists, not dwelling on the negative but seeing the positive possibilities and utilizing them to their fullest. For the self-actualizer, life was meaningful and worth while.

There are obviously many parallels between Maslow's 'self-actualizer' and someone developing towards Maharishi's fifth state of consciousness. Apart from the obvious semantic similarity between self-actualization and Self-realization, most of the characteristics of self-actualizers are also those which Maharishi claims for the Self-realized person. These similarities are borne out by psychological tests on TM subjects. Questionnaires have been developed to test the degree to which a person is a 'self-actualizer'. One such test (Shostram's Personal Orientation Inventory) was given to a group of university students before learning the TM technique and then again two months later. The results were compared with those of a control group who were given the same test but did not start the TM technique. Bearing in mind the caution with which one should approach all questionnaire studies the results are none the less interesting. Compared to the control group, the meditating subjects showed a significant movement in the direction of self-actualization – and this within only two months of learning the TM technique.[2] This tendency has been confirmed by other tests,[3] and is supported by several studies which show a movement away from neuroticism,[4] depression,[5] and anxiety[6] towards a state of increased psychological health.

Of Peaks and Plateaux

One of Maslow's most interesting findings was that self-actualizers tended to have a high frequency of 'Peak-experiences'. These he described as 'moments of great awe ... pure, positive happiness, when all doubts, all fears, all inhibitions, all weaknesses were left behind', in which one felt 'one was the world, pleased with it, really belonging to it, instead of being outside looking in ... the feeling that they had really seen the ultimate truth, the essence of things. ...'[7]

The existence of such experiences was not, of course, a new discovery: mystics, poets and other 'gifted' people had often reported them. But Maslow found that their occurrence was not limited to any particular group of people; they occurred just as much among businessmen, industrialists, managers, educators and political people as among the professionally 'religious', the poets, musicians, and others who were supposed to have such experiences.

One might ask whether peak experiences are related to any of Maharishi's higher states of consciousness? Clearly a peak experience is not the same as transcendental consciousness for in a peak experience one is usually enraptured by something whereas in pure transcendental consciousness there is no object of awareness. There remains the possibility that a peak experience may be a temporary glimpse of cosmic consciousness. In a few cases the descriptions of peak experiences do sound remarkably similar, but in general the term is used to cover such a wide range of experience – almost any ecstatic experience could count as a peak experience – that it would be extremely dangerous to equate the two.

If there is any trace of Maharishi's higher states of consciousness in Maslow's work it is probably to be found in the 'plateau experience' with which he became very involved in the later years of his life. Plateau experiences were something like continuous peak experiences but without the suddenness or excitement of the peak experience. He describes a plateau experience as a 'witnessing, an appreciating, what one might call a serene, cognitive blissfulness'.[8] Unfortunately, Maslow died shortly after he began work on the plateau experience and it is impossible to tell from the descriptions he did give whether or not they do represent glimpses of Maharishi's fifth state of consciousness.

Even though it may not be possible to equate peak and plateau experiences with higher states of consciousness, the fact that the TM technique leads to an increase in self-actualization would lead us to expect that the growth towards a higher state of consciousness would be accompanied by a higher frequency of these experiences.

Metapathology

Alan Watts points out in *Psychotherapy East and West* that Western therapeutic techniques tend to concentrate only on those with very dramatic or peculiar disturbances, the most unfortunate sufferers in our society, whereas the Eastern approaches to therapy are concerned with improving the lot of everyone. What we regard as normal is in fact far below man's full potential, it is in effect a state of psychological impoverishment. This impoverishment, he writes, is the origin and breeding-ground of much mental disease.

Carl Jung appears to have held similar views. He felt that all men had a fundamental need for inner development and an understanding of the meaning and significance of life. The lack of satisfaction of this need was, he believed, the root of many of man's 'neuro-psychic' disorders.

Maslow saw a similar relationship between psychological health and self-actualization. He believed that human needs were arranged in a hierarchical structure. Needs lower down the hierarchy, such as the need for food and oxygen, dominate until a sufficient level of satisfaction is reached and then the next level of need emerges, in this case the need for group esteem which in

Western societies usually appears as the need for material possessions. The fifth level of need is the need for self-actualization, for growth, health and full humanness. Maslow called this a 'metaneed' in contrast to the other more basic needs. In the same way that deprivation of any of the more basic needs leads to physical and mental illness of one kind or another so deprivation of metaneeds leads to what he calls 'metapathology', a state characterized by cynicism, nihilism, hatred, bleakness, disintegration, boredom, hopelessness, insecurity, selfishness, confusion, conflict, depression and boredom – 'a sickness of the soul'. The fact that we see the symptoms of metapathology all around us shows that our society does not yet provide a reliable or effective means of fulfilling metaneeds. One might conclude that what is needed is some form of 'metatherapy'.

Daniel Goleman defines a metatherapy as 'a procedure that accomplishes the major goals of conventional therapy and yet has as its end-state a change far beyond the scope of therapies, therapists, and most personality theorists – an altered state of consciousness'.[9] The Transcendental Meditation program clearly satisfies these criteria. Goleman himself suggests that just as behaviour therapy and psychoanalysis were the tools of the second force in psychology, and encounter groups the tool of humanistic psychology, so meditation may be the main vehicle for the rapidly emerging fourth school, what is often known as Transpersonal Psychology.

Transpersonal Psychology, as its name implies, is concerned with those aspects of experience which take a person beyond individuality. Its principal studies are 'ecstasy, mystical experience, being, essence, bliss, awe, wonder, self-actualization, self-transcendence, spirit, sacralization of everyday life, oneness, cosmic awareness . . .'.[10] Although it would be a mistake to equate the transpersonal with the transcendental, transpersonal psychology at present represents the closest approach that psychology has made to the study of higher states of consciousness. This can be seen from the following passage from Roberto Assagioli, one of the principal figures behind this movement:[11]

> The changing *contents* of our consciousness (the sensations, thoughts, feelings, etc.) are one thing, while the 'I', the self, the *center* of our consciousness is another. From a certain point of view this difference can be compared to that existing

between the white lighted area on a cinema screen and the various pictures which are projected upon it.

But the 'man in the street' and even many well-educated people do not take the trouble to observe themselves and to discriminate; they drift on the surface of the 'mind-stream' and identify themselves with its successive waves, with the changing contents of their consciousness.

Assagioli similarly believes that this mistaken identity results in unnecessary emotional conflicts and desires, leading to misery and suffering, and a society which is continually at loggerheads with itself. It is, he believes, one of the goals of life to be aware of the Self in whatever one is doing.

Thus far he is largely in agreement with Maharishi, but a major difference arises when it comes to the actual techniques used for developing Self-realization. In order to bring about the synthesis of the pure Self with the normal stream of consciousness Assagioli has developed a system of personal development known as 'psychosynthesis'. (He uses this term in contradistinction to psychoanalysis – although, as he himself remarks, much of Jungian analytic psychology embodied synthetic principles.) Psychosynthesis involves a large variety of practices, some of them working on the physical level (e.g. body awareness, dance and music); others working on the psychological level (e.g. self observation, dream analysis, imagery). Without doubt many of these techniques do have a significant effect on both physical and mental health and are of great benefit to the individual, but it is not immediately apparent that they will also lead to transcendental consciousness. This difference between Maharishi and Assagioli is reflected in the above quotation, where Assagioli appears to be more concerned with *remembering* the Self, 'observing' and 'discriminating', rather than coming to a state of pure Self-awareness. There is always the danger that such practices may cultivate only an idea of the Self as a *content* of consciousness rather than the direct knowledge of it as the *center* of consciousness.

Chemical Transformations of Consciousness

There is a feeling among some psychologists, and among many non-psychologists, that it is possible to induce higher states of consciousness by directly changing the brain chemistry.

Surprisingly Maharishi agrees with this in principle. Since a higher state of consciousness is dependent upon a specific mode of functioning of the nervous system it should in theory be possible to bring about the necessary modifications in function by a chemical modification of the nervous system. But, he adds, none of the chemicals that we have at our disposal today produce the correct changes – indeed their effects are often in the opposite direction.

Not all mystical-sounding experiences are necessarily of a mystical nature. When it comes to describing inner states of consciousness our language is very limited and one may often be forced to use the same phrase to describe very different experiences. Thus a mere verbal description of two states is not always sufficient to differentiate them.

To take a specific example, LSD tends to be concentrated in the visual system of the brain. By a process of selective inhibition it increases visual activity resulting in the legendary enhancement of color and pattern. In effect what was previously random noise in the system is now reaching consciousness. When this is very strong one may well have experiences in which white light seems to pervade all that is seen. Comparing this experience with similar descriptions of the sixth state of consciousness one might easily assume that the two were identical. But when both states are experienced rather than just described it immediately becomes clear how very different they are.

Similarly it is quite possible for drugs to produce states of consciousness in which the perceiver and the perceived become one. But this is a very different state of unity to that reached in the seventh state of consciousness. In the drug-induced state the union usually arises through a loss of distinction; one loses oneself in the experience. But in the true experience of unity there is no loss of distinction; the perceiver and the perceived remain clearly differentiated. Added to this normal awareness is the awareness of an underlying oneness which transcends all boundaries. Not unity at the expense of diversity, but unity in addition to all diversity.

Furthermore the drug-induced state is usually of a transient nature. The body soon rids itself of the foreign material and returns to the normal waking state leaving only a memory of another reality; and a memory, however strong, is not the same as a change in consciousness.

For many people drugs have often had the effect of opening a person's awareness to the possibility of some higher state of consciousness – even if they did not actually provide it. In this respect drugs may in some cases have served as a stepping stone, albeit a slippery and treacherous one. But having crossed the stream the stepping stone is finished with: if it is carried on it only becomes an impediment to further progress.

Many people who have been engaged in drug-taking report that after starting the TM program their drug usage decreases. Several surveys have already been carried out to see how far these claims can be substantiated. The largest survey to date covered 1,862 meditators, and the results indicate a general and dramatic decrease in all types of drug usage.[12]

Figure 13 *Decrease in use of non-prescribed drugs in people practising the TM technique (taken from Benson and Wallace's survey of 1,862 meditators).*

These general tendencies have been confirmed by the several other projects which have been conducted in this field.[13]

Most subjects confirmed that with the TM program life became more enjoyable and the need for drugs decreased. One subject reported that he had 'no need for drugs any more for I have found what life is and how I want to live it'. Another that 'life after meditation finally became satisfying'. And a third that 'I didn't try to stop – after a while I just found myself not taking them any more.' Many found the drug experience to be less satisfactory, with such comments as: '[The] drug effect interfered with the good effects of meditation', drugs 'proved temporarily dulling and moody' and 'I have no desire to become disorientated or to be unclear in my thoughts.'[14]

Partly because of the negative side-effects of drugs and partly because of their social and political implications the governments of most Western countries make great effects to eliminate them. This, however, is only eradicating the symptoms of the problem. If the need is still there people will simply find other chemical means to their goals – and probably more dangerous ones at that. If the problem is to be permanently resolved and not just patched up each time that it reappears one must attend to the root of the problem.

A large number of the people now experimenting with drugs of one kind or another are doing so as part of a search for some higher state of consciousness and a more meaningful perspective of reality. The root cause of the problem is not the availability of the drug or the social conditions which promote its use but the absence of any alternative means to raise the level of consciousness. Rather than fruitlessly trying to eliminate drugs themselves governments should be turning their attention to providing more acceptable and less damaging ways of allowing people to fulfil these needs.

The Adulation of Childhood

Because both the enlightened person and the very young child experience a certain oneness with the world it is sometimes suggested that enlightenment may be returning to a state of mental functioning similar to that of early childhood. Psychologists call such a return to an earlier level of functioning 'regression' and have tried to explain higher states of consciousness in terms of this phenomenon. But, as with those who draw parallels between mystical experiences and drug experiences, the similarities between enlightenment and regression are very superficial and tend to reflect the inadequacy of our language rather than the similarity of the states.

The enlightened state is one of *differentiated union*: the world is known for all its diversity *and* for its essential unity with the Self. With the young child, on the other hand, the state tends to be one of *undifferentiated unity*: the ego has not yet attained any degree of autonomy and the child fails to recognize any distinction between his individual self and the rest of the world. The first is a state of knowledge resulting from a full experience of reality: the second a state of relative ignorance arising from a lack of experience.

It is true that many enlightened men have a certain child-like quality about them, but it is not so much a return to childhood that one is witnessing as a fuller maturity which synthesizes the innocence and openness of childhood with the experience and wisdom of adulthood. Not a circle from unity to diversity and back to unity: but a spiral from unity through diversity to an awareness of unity and diversity together. In most cases higher states of consciousness have led to a transformation of the individual in the direction of wholeness, health and self-actualization. And the healthier that a person becomes the more optimistic is his attitude, the less self-centered his actions and the more meaningful his life – qualities not usually found in infantile regression.

The Means and the Ends

13

Liberation can be achieved neither by physical postures, nor by speculative philosophy, nor by religious ceremonies, nor by mere learning ... Let people quote the scriptures and sacrifice to the gods, let them perform rituals and worship the deities, but there is no liberation without the realization of one's identity with the Self.

Shankara

A higher state of consciousness is in essence an inner change, but with this inner change come many changes in one's outer life. Observing this people have often sought to cultivate the ways of an enlightened person in the belief that they will thereby raise their own level of consciousness. But this is to confuse the *results* of a changed state of consciousness for its *cause*. It is putting the cart before the horse and in many cases results in a cart with no horse at all.

The way an enlightened person speaks and acts is the result of his inner development; to try and achieve the same state by copying him is rather like a poor person trying to get rich by copying the behaviour of a wealthy one. The wealthy person can buy this or that at will, but the poor person who imitates his style of living ends up further than ever from the goal. A person must first raise his level of consciousness then, *as a result*, he will spontaneously develop the qualities of an enlightened person.

Self-Remembering

One common error is the attempt to remember the Self on the level of thinking. Understanding that the Self-realized person has an awareness of the true inner Self, many have believed that by deliberately trying to 'remember themselves' as a conscious *idea* they will develop this inner awareness. Gurdjieff, for example, declared this to be one intention of his system: 'We copy the effects of consciousness,' he said, 'in order that they will stay with us.' His followers have tried to maintain the experience of the Self by thinking about it, by trying to hold on to an idea of the Self throughout daily activity. But whatever it is that is being remembered, being an idea of some kind, cannot be the true Self. Moreover, the more that one concentrates on any idea the stronger that activity becomes and the more that it overshadows the real Self.

Such practices may well produce a witnessing experience, but it is not the same as that which comes with a higher state of consciousness. In the fifth state of consciousness the Self is a witness to all activity, but the witnessing which these practices lead to is a mental activity in which one is conscious *of* something. 'I am conscious of myself looking at the flower.' 'I am witnessing myself doing this and doing that.' This is not a separation between the pure Self and all activity, physical and mental: only a separation between part of the mind and the rest of experience and activity.

Merely understanding or thinking about an experience will never by itself bring about that experience. It may be true that 'the Self is a witness to all activity', but merely maintaining this as an intellectual idea will never bring about the changes of consciousness which will allow this understanding to become a living reality.

No person ever escaped from a prison, either mental or physical, by thinking about escape or repeating to himself that he was free. It may have given some the encouragement to get down to doing something about it, but by itself it can only result in delusion: a freedom which disappears as soon as one falls asleep and stops thinking about it.

Rather than leading to an integrated and strengthened personality such conscious remembering of one's self divides the attention and weakens the mind. Half the mind is involved in looking after normal activity and sensory experience, and half the mind is involved in self-remembering. Activity suffers because it is not receiving one's full attention, while Self-awareness remains an empty idea. One loses out both ways and ends up further than ever from a state of enlightened fulfilment.

A recent variation of this theme suggests that while eating a meal you should continually remind yourself of every action involved in the process. It is believed that by destroying any enjoyment there might be in eating the person will be left as a mere witness to the act of eating. It certainly does destroy all enjoyment; as the commentator himself remarked, 'By the time you are half way through the meal you've got the screaming meemies.'[1] Even if you were to survive the 'screaming meemies' the process would again leave you witnessing only on the level of thinking, not on the level of pure consciousness. In addition it would not even be an imitation of cosmic consciousness, for the Self-realized person both witnesses *and* enjoys.

Imitations of Immortality

Another common form of imitation is the attempt to copy the words and actions of an enlightened person. This may well seem even more ridiculous, but it is, nevertheless, very widespread. How many people leading a 'good life' are doing so not solely for the joy which it will bring to themselves and to others, but also with the hope that by helping others they will raise their own level of consciousness, or reap some other spiritual reward?

Now I am not suggesting that we should not be helping others, but we should not expect that by doing so we will raise our level of consciousness. Indeed to indulge in 'self-less' behaviour in order to raise one's level of consciousness will usually lead to an identification with one's own sense of goodness. Bondage to experience becomes even stronger and true Self-realization moves even further away.

Furthermore, how are we to know whether the right action for the enlightened person in one situation will necessarily be the right action for us in our own situation? Out of its true context it may be most inappropriate and damaging, not just to us but to others and our environment as well.

At other times people have tried to imitate the physiology of what they take to be an enlightened person, but with little more success and often with disastrous consequences. It may be found that people in higher states of consciousness eat only certain foods and then only in certain quantities – presumably because their physiological needs have changed. But forcing such a diet on an unprepared body will quickly lead to malnutrition. It may well produce an altered state of consciousness but it certainly is not a prerequisite to enlightenment. 'A healthy mind in a healthy body!'

Similar inversions occur with the breathing. It has often been claimed that in the state of *samadhi* (transcendental consciousness) the breath stops completely and for considerable periods of time – a claim which recent experiments appear to be substantiating. But it is pretty certain that were an ordinary person to hold his breath for ten or fifteen minutes he would reach a very different type of *samadhi*!

No enlightened person ever had to control his body, his actions, his words or his thoughts; if they changed they changed as a spontaneous result of his higher state of consciousness. We can only act as we are – it is what we are that must change.

The Four Aspects of Yoga

Although he has himself come from India, Maharishi's teaching differs significantly from contemporary teachings of Yoga. He believes that the plethora of practices which today pass under the title of 'Yoga' are descended from one common source, but as always the passage of time has caused the original teaching to become distorted and misunderstood. Consequently we now have a variety of systems which often bear little obvious relation either to each other or to their common origin.

Traditionally the techniques of Yoga are divided into four principal categories: Raja Yoga (which includes Hatha Yoga) means the Royal Yoga and is concerned with various forms of meditation and techniques of purification of the nervous system; Karma Yoga is the path of action; Bhakti Yoga the path of devotion; and Gyana Yoga the path of knowledge. Each of these systems comprises a complex philosophical and metaphysical framework and a wide range of practices. It is therefore impossible to do each justice in such a brief summary. There are also many minor systems of Yoga: some are separate systems in their own right; some are subsystems of the four major systems; and some are eclectic systems which have taken selections of techniques from the other systems. But as far as we are concerned here any practice which achieves the goal of Unity Consciousness may be classed as Yoga.

Maharishi takes the view that the four major systems of Yoga were not originally different paths to enlightenment but represented different aspects of enlightenment. The fully enlightened person is one who maintains transcendental consciousness throughout his activity; he is a Raja Yogi. He no longer identifies with his actions and as a result they are more in accord with the needs of nature; a Karma Yogi. His heart expresses supreme devotion to the whole of creation; a Bhakti Yogi. And he knows as a matter of direct personal experience that the Self is, in essence, identical with the rest of creation; a Gyana Yogi. But when the natural path to Unity was lost all that remained were descriptions of the effects of Yoga. The unenlightened person once again began to copy the effects of consciousness and the four principal consequences of reaching the goal were seen as four different paths to it.

Maharishi cites many instances of how the original yogic teachings appear to have become inverted over the ages and the effects taken for the cause. In many traditions, for example, it is now taught that inner purity is a prerequisite to enlightenment and that one must practise righteous living before even being allowed to meditate. But inner purity and righteous living are the effects of gaining enlightenment. Meditation itself purifies the individual, as a snowplough clears its own way, leaving a clear path behind it as the *effect* of its action. Trying to purify the system first in order that the 'way to the Self' may be clear is like walking ahead of the snowplough shovelling all the snow out of the way first in order that the snowplough may have a clear run. You may still reach the goal but it is a far more lengthy and arduous procedure, and moreover, it is tragic waste of a most powerful tool.

200 per cent of Life

In the East the ascetic approach to life has been supported by the idea that since 'all this is in truth One' the various forms which the 'all this' takes must be an illusion. The physical world has come to be ignored, or in some cases even despised, and fulfilment has been seen solely in spiritual terms – often with disastrous consequences. Conversely, the apparently successful materialist-behaviourist paradigm has led us in the West to ignore, and sometimes even despise, the possibility of an inner development, with the result that fulfilment has been seen in predominantly material terms – and with equally disastrous consequences.

Maharishi's apparently revolutionary teaching is that inner and outer fulfilment are both possible; that one can live a full spiritual life along with a full material one. It is neither necessary nor advantageous to retire from the material world in order to reap the rewards of an inner development. Nor, conversely, is it possible to fully enjoy the delights of the physical world without an equal inner enrichment. The two support each other. Inner satisfaction enhances outer progress and outer satisfaction enhances inner progress.

To live life in fulfilment, Maharishi emphasizes, is to live 200 per cent of life – 100 per cent inner life plus 100 per cent outer life; a full spiritual life along with a full material life; full appreciation of the absolute along with full enjoyment of the relative. The fully enlightened person has a fully developed heart and a fully developed mind; love and reason, so often held to be in opposition, are now found coexisting in harmony. The balance between the two 'opposing' modes of thought having been restored thinking is not active *or* receptive but active *and* receptive; intellectual *and* intuitive; scientific *and* artistic; concrete *and* abstract; focal *and* diffuse; – a synthesis of all polarities.

This synthesis is the result of a fundamental change in consciousness. It is not the same as trying to think of opposites simultaneously: that would simply overload the left half of the brain even more heavily. If any success at all were achieved in this direction it would probably only amount to the ability to maintain a 'happy medium' between the opposing ideas. The balancing of opposites experienced by the enlightened person is not a compromise of opposites: it is a true synthesis of opposites in which both are enjoyed to the full and neither is appeased. The enlightened person does not stand midway between a material and a spiritual life: he lives both to the full as aspects of a higher reality – a *dynamic* balancing of opposites.

Roberto Assagioli illustrates this point by the use of a triangle:[2] the two base corners represent the opposing polarities, and their midpoint is the happy medium. The true synthesis is the apex of the triangle; a higher reality encompassing both of the opposites in their fullnesses. Figure 14 shows Assagioli's example of the opposites sympathy and antipathy with their compromise and synthesis.

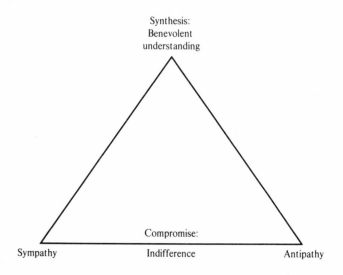

Figure 14 *Assagioli's triangle demonstrating the difference between compromise and synthesis of opposites. Similar diagrams could be drawn for most other polarities of human thought.*

Nearly all the spiritual teachers have made reference to this synthesis of opposites making it one of the hallmarks of enlightenment. The Middle Way of Buddhism, for example, is, according to Christmas Humphreys,[3] not 'a weak compromise but a living synthesis, a creative moving forward in which the opposites are consumed, digested and made one'.

Much of alchemy can be seen as the attempt to realize the co-existence of opposites in a symbolic manner. In the 'chymical wedding' the union was symbolized by the amalgam. The attempt to produce an amalgam of iron and copper, for example, may seem misconceived today, but when we remember that iron and copper correspond to Mars and Venus and that these in turn represented the male and female aspects of creation then the picture becomes clearer. To form an amalgam was to unite symbolically the opposing male and female poles of the universe, and the result was the creation of gold, a symbolic return to the enlightened state.

As symbolic expressions of the synthesis these accounts are fascinating, but it would be unwise to take them as a means to enlightenment for this would once again be putting the cart before the horse. The only way to achieve this union personally is to first raise one's level of consciousness, then 'all these things shall be added unto you'.

The Knower and the Known

14

A University is a place where the universality of the human spirit manifests itself.

Albert Einstein

Contemporary education is frequently criticized because the knowledge which is taught bears little obvious relationship to the students' own experience or to the situations they are likely to encounter when they leave school. This does not necessarily mean that the knowledge taught is wrong – it may be entirely correct – but it is not always entirely relevant or useful. Alvin Toffler points out in *Future Shock* that the curriculum today is more concerned with what was of use yesterday than with what will be of use tomorrow, 'a mindless holdover from the past'.[1]

In most cases our present educational system is concerned with the development of the rational aspect of the mind: the 'intuitive' aspect of the mind remains relatively undeveloped. The result is an impressive collection of facts and highly developed powers of reason but little sense of value. Without a sense of value a person has no way of judging whether or not they are applying their intellect to a good end. Reason will tell them the outcome of their actions but not whether such an outcome is right or wrong. In order to develop a sense of value it is necessary to develop the emotional and intuitive side of the person along with their rationality. This requires the development of a deeper awareness and an integration of both aspects of the mind. By largely ignoring these aspects of the individual contemporary education leaves the development of a sense of value up to the parents, or, if they fail, up to the students themselves. Most parents and students, however, have little idea of how best to achieve such a development and so we turn out people with prodigious powers of reasoning and argument but very little feeling or sense of value: A. N. Whitehead's 'merely well informed man' who 'is the most useless bore on God's earth'.[2]

So often a mere barrage of facts leads not to the development of the mind but to its death. Einstein, recalling his own education, commented: 'One had to cram all this stuff into one's mind, whether one liked it or not. This coercion had such a deterring effect that, after I had passed the final examination, I found the consideration of any scientific problems distasteful for one entire year.'[3]

It is sometimes thought that this can be remedied by making the facts more interesting and relevant. But this alone is not enough. The students' ability to appreciate a fact depends upon the level of his or her awareness. A dull mind may see some item as merely another boring fact, whereas a clear alert mind may see a greater significance in it and be able to relate it to other knowledge. This is the very first point that Aldous Huxley makes in *The Perennial Philosophy*: 'Knowledge is a function of Being. When there is a change in the Being of the knower, there is a corresponding change in the nature and the amount of knowing.'[4] But, as he points out in a later essay,[5] present education refuses to accept increased inner development as either possible or useful. It has become so concerned with filling the mind that it has no time to consider the development of awareness or the direct expansion of the mind.

In an attempt to do something practical about these failings, Maharishi has sanctioned the founding of the Maharishi International University (MIU). Its intention is to develop the student's awareness along with the assimilation of information. This is achieved by incorporating the study and practice of the TM technique as an integral part of the curriculum. The student at

MIU follows similar academic courses as he would at any other university, and added to these is the Science of Creative Intelligence (SCI), which is defined as 'the systematic study of the nature, origin, range, and application of creative intelligence in life'. SCI explores the implications of the TM technique in depth. The actual practice of the technique becomes an experiment by which theoretical hypotheses about 'the nature, origin, range and application of creative intelligence in individual life' can be tested. As we shall see shortly SCI introduces a whole new approach to interdisciplinary studies.

The motto of MIU is 'Knowledge is structured in consciousness'. This could almost have come straight from Huxley but in fact it comes from the Rig Veda of ancient India. The use of the word 'structure' in this context is sometimes puzzling. Roughly interpreted we might take the phrase to mean that consciousness is the medium in which knowledge takes form. To know anything at all a person first has to be conscious and the degree to which he is conscious affects the depth of his knowledge. An unconscious person knows nothing; a partially conscious person (one in the waking state) has a partial knowledge of reality; a fully conscious person, one with full awareness of his own inner nature and of the external world, has a full knowledge of reality. Thus the higher the level of consciousness the more profound the level of knowledge.

Objective and Subjective Knowledge

When we talk of knowledge or truth we are referring to those aspects of the world and of our experience which are unchanging. We know that something is true if under a wide variety of conditions we arrive at the same conclusions. Experience itself is not knowledge because experience consists only of change; all the information supplied by the senses to the brain is concerned with changes in the external world. The process of gaining knowledge is in essence the process of abstracting unchanging features from our ever-changing experience. When we see a tree, for example, the eyes only tell us of continually changing patches of brown and green (continually changing because the eye is never still). But the changes are found to possess a certain order: they have a well-defined boundary and a certain internal structure. The senses do not tell of this, our brains abstract this orderliness and on this basis we arrive at the concept of a tree.

We might say that experience is born of the interaction between the object of perception, 'the thing in itself', and the subject of perception, the transcendental Self. Now although experience itself is always changing the pure subject and the pure object remain invariable – and hence lie beyond sensory experience. The search for knowledge can therefore take either of two possible directions: one may try to discover the invariant nature of the object; or one may try to discover the invariant nature of the subject. These two approaches could be said to represent the objective and the subjective approaches.

In order for knowledge to qualify as truth it must be agreed upon by all people at all times. The objective approach tries to achieve this by eliminating as far as possible the variations introduced by the internal state of the observer. This is the principle of objectivity and is the basis of Western science. The subjective approach, on the other hand, tries to achieve consistency by establishing a state of consciousness which is the same for everyone and unperturbed by changes in the external world. This involves the development of a full awareness of the Self which is maintained throughout all experience, i.e. the development of Self-realization.

The objective and the subjective approaches to knowledge may look very different on the surface but deep down they are remarkably similar. The more that Western science delves into the finer levels of creation the more that statements of the scientist come to resemble those of mystics who have reached the same level of knowledge through a subjective investigation of reality.

On the surface, however, the objective and subjective paths remain very different and in this respect are only partially useful and fulfilling. If knowledge is to be complete then a synthesis of these two approaches is required: a synthesis in which neither approach compromises the other but both coexist together as two separate aspects of a single holistic path of knowledge. MIU sees this being achieved through the introduction of the TM program into the regular curriculum. By gaining greater Self-awareness and inner stability the student at MIU should be able to draw upon subjective experience without interference from the outside world and also be able to examine the outer world without interference from the inside – full subjective stability along with full objective reliability. This is what Maharishi refers to as 'full knowledge'. He does not mean that a person should have a detailed knowledge of every field of life – that is clearly impossible – but that he should have a full knowledge of some specialist field of inquiry along with a full knowledge of his own inner nature.

He believes that 'the natural result of sustained exposure to *full* education is the development of permanently broadened awareness and the establishment of a state of consciousness that expresses the ideals of human strength, compassion, stability, creativity, and fulfilment.'[6]

SCI and Interdisciplinary Studies

The word 'university' is derived from the Latin word *universitas* meaning wholeness or, more literally, 'turned into one'. The early medieval universities tried to achieve this holistic ideal by teaching Theology, Common Law and Mathematics together. But the explosive growth in both the complexity and range of knowledge has since made increasing degrees of specialization a necessity. Such fragmentation is, however, highly artificial. Life does not fall easily into such well-defined compartments as the specialist would like and many of the fields overlap considerably. Indeed, the more one comes to specialize in any particular field the more one begins to find oneself drawing on other widely separated specialist disciplines. The neuro-psychologist, for example, may find that he must call upon such disciplines as biochemistry, quantum physics, physiology, cybernetics and mathematics, as well as possessing the skills of a competent electronic engineer and computer programmer. It is partly as an attempt to fulfil this need for a more general education that there has recently been an expanding interest in inter-disciplinary studies.

The predominant approach to inter-disciplinary studies has been concerned with trying to establish common domains between the various fields of knowledge. It is easy, for example, to trace links between physics and chemistry, chemistry and physiology, physiology and psychology, and on through psychology to sociology, anthropology, comparative religion, philosophy, mathematics, and back again to physics. But this only establishes the surface interrelationships between the different disciplines: not their fundamental basis.

What is common to all the different fields of study is a search for order. Every discipline seeks to discover these aspects of its field which are invariable, and by so doing make another contribution to our knowledge of the Universe.

As the tree of knowledge has grown it has branched out in many different directions, and these branches have themselves divided and subdivided into ever more minute fractions of the whole. We have now become so preoccupied with the tips of the branches and the fruits which they bear that the trunk of the tree has been almost entirely obscured and forgotten. So when it comes to studying the interrelationships of the various disciplines we look at them on the level of the leaf, comparing their superficial similarities and interconnections rather than their common underlying basis. Consequently students have come to regard interdisciplinary studies as superficial, and 'general studies' as something of a light relief from the real business of in-depth study.

The approach at MIU is very different. Through the practical aspect of the Science of Creative Intelligence (i.e. the TM technique), the student is gaining a direct personal experience of pure creative intelligence and hence of the basic ordering principle of nature. He is therefore following the subjective path of knowledge right back to the trunk. But since this is the same trunk from which all the objective branches of knowledge have also sprung he gains a familiarity at a very fundamental level with all fields of study. His awareness being open to 'cosmic intelligence' he begins to feel as if 'in tune' with all the different disciplines, an experience which Maharishi refers to as 'being at home with all the branches of knowledge'.

Now this does not mean that a man who has never studied quantum physics, for example, will spontaneously come by a detailed knowledge of the subject: he will still have to study the subject in depth if he is to gain this sort of information. But when he does study the subject he will find himself 'at home' with it and better able to assimilate the detailed facts and theories involved.

In Figure 15 I have depicted a selection of interconnected disciplines as lying around the perimeter of a circle, each discipline merging into the next as, for example, physics merges into chemistry in the field of molecular structure. The present superficial approach to interdisciplinary studies tries to relate one subject to another by seeing the surface interconnections round the perimeter of the circle. If we let the center of the circle represent the field of pure creative intelligence, the inner core of all these various disciplines, then the Science of Creative In-

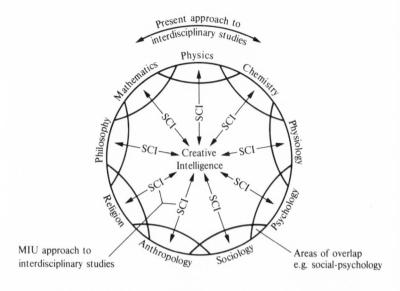

Figure 15 *A selection of different studies showing their rela-
tedness to each other and to SCI, and the corresponding approaches to interdisciplinary studies.*

telligence becomes an interface between the direct experience of
transcendental consciousness and the study of specific fields of
knowledge. With this basis, all the various disciplines come to be
perceived as aspects of a whole.

SCI and Science

In the past the study of states of consciousness has been largely
confined to the East with the result that most people in the West
have come to regard the whole field as 'oriental' and therefore
alien to their own science. In many cases their study has come to
be regarded as positively unscientific, and, in a derogatory sense,
mystical. Maharishi has progressively removed the embellishments
of the Orient to show that these teachings can be expressed and
understood just as satisfactorily, if not more satisfactorily, in
Western terms as in Eastern ones. By deliberately referring to the
study of creative intelligence as a science, he is trying to make
people continually aware that inner development and the evolution of consciousness can be analysed as objectively and rationally
as any other subject. Its claims are open to test through personal

and public experiment and must be accepted or rejected on this basis.

It might be objected that SCI is not scientific because much of it is concerned with the changes which occur in higher states of consciousness and that only a person who was himself in a higher state could verify the hypotheses. But this criticism could equally be applied to most 'orthodox' sciences. We accept the theories of atomic physicists, for example, because they have been borne out by other experts in the field. We do not ask that we have a billion dollar cyclotron in our back garden: we put our faith in others who are recognized as authorities in the field, accepting that in principle at least we could duplicate the experiments. The results of SCI are also, in principle, duplicatable by anyone. Since the TM process does not depend on an individual's personality, character or intellectual ability but on the structure of the normal thinking process anyone can practise the technique and test the claims of SCI. If other people in, or on the way to, higher states of consciousness support Maharishi's propositions then that should be sufficient validation for the layman.

The title itself is not as important as whether or not it works and is of value. Philosophers of science still argue about whether sociology, for example, is worthy of the title science. Yet, while they continue their deliberations, sociology continues to provide deeper insights into the functioning of individuals within society.

Nor do we need to understand the theoretical framework of the subject in order for it to be valuable. Most of us do not know the physical principles which underlie the functioning of a simple transistor – indeed, if they were explained to us we would probably refuse to believe them for the theories of quantum physics often appear in direct contradiction to our everyday experience – yet we accept transistors, and the resultant electronic gadgetry not because we understand them but because they work. Likewise, even if some of the concepts behind SCI initially seem to be as far removed from everyday life as quantum theory is, we should still judge its merits on whether or not it works and is useful.

Maharishi International University

The study of creative intelligence is the keystone of study at MIU. At whatever level a student may enter MIU, whether it be from high school or at the Ph.D. level, he takes the same basic introductory course for one year. This starts with a one-month course on SCI, and then, with this basis, he moves on to an interdisciplinary study which gives a basic introduction to a number of different subjects and examines their fundamental principles in the light of SCI. Now it is obviously impossible for the student to go into a detailed study of each field in so short a time, but the purpose of these courses is to relate the basic principles of each subject to the basic principles of SCI – to see the different branches of knowledge not merely as branches, but as branches emanating from a common trunk. It is only after this very broad and basic framework is established that a student begins to specialize in his chosen field. And when he does come to specialize he receives as deep and as rigorous treatment of his field as he would at any other university.

By incorporating Self-knowledge into its educational system, MIU is not just adding subjective knowledge but is paving the way to a better objective knowledge as well. Students at MIU have reported that the study of different disciplines becomes much easier and more interesting and pilot studies carried out on meditating students have supported this claim by showing that there was a significant all-round improvement in academic performance.[7]

The curriculum at MIU includes a month of 'residential vacation' once every three months. During this period students undertake no formal studies, but instead retire to what are called 'forest academies'. These are retreats located well away from the cities and university, and during his stay there the student has a chance to gain a deeper personal experience of the Transcendental Meditation technique. Such periods of rest are intended to accelerate the 'purification of the nervous system', and allow the student to gain sustained experience of the finer levels of thought. The net effect is an enhancement in the rate of personal evolution and the development of consciousness.

As any student knows, the assimilation of knowledge takes place in those moments of complete relaxation when one is not busy studying. By structuring these long periods of deep rest into the course, MIU also gives the student a real chance to digest and order the knowledge he has gained.

Another unique part of the MIU curriculum is the inclusion of extended periods of field-work. A postgraduate student at MIU will probably spend half his time out of the university learning to apply his specialist knowledge in the world, directly experiencing the relationship of his specialist field of study with the needs of society, and learning to apply his understanding in real life. This both crystallizes his knowledge, and tests its validity in the context of life in society. Students at MIU should not therefore be complaining that their studies have little relevance to real life.

The reaction from students to the setting up of MIU has been very enthusiastic. Encouraged by the promise of a 'coherent, unified, progressively illuminating, purposeful', education, 'directly supportive of personal growth' offering 'rapid release of stress, richness of experience, and depth of knowledge',[8] many students who had previously dropped out of the conventional universities are coming back and signing up again. The students, at least, would appear to appreciate that MIU is filling a gap in the present educational system.

MIU has already received official recognition in the United States and has been running regular courses there since 1973. In 1974 it moved from its provisional campus in Santa Barbara, California, to a larger permanent site at Fairfield, Iowa. At the same time research laboratories were set up in New York and Switzerland. In addition the faculty staff have recorded the bulk of the MIU courses on video-tape so that students can take the courses in their own countries at local TM centers. Eventually the courses will be extended to cover education at the secondary and primary school levels, and at the adult level, in order that full personal development can 'be made available to all men and women of every age-group, every interest, every background and every degree of educational involvement'.[9]

Transcending all these goals is Maharishi's intention to establish a more permanent foundation for the TM program. MIU he hopes will not only spread the TM technique widely across the world but also leave behind such a firm understanding of the underlying principles that distortion and misunderstandings will in future find it much harder to creep in.

Part Three

Part One looked at how the TM technique, by giving deep rest to the whole organism, dissolved deep-rooted stresses resulting in a healthier body and clearer, more alert mind. Part Two showed how, with this increased clarity of mind, one begins to unfold the pure Self underlying all mental activity. This formed the basis of several higher states of consciousness. In transcendental consciousness, reached during the TM technique when the mind is completely still, one is aware of the pure Self alone. Through the regular alternation of the TM technique and normal daily activity a stage is reached in which awareness of the pure Self is maintained throughout the day. This is the fifth state of consciousness. Further development entails the gradual refinement of one's perception of the outside world until finally in the seventh state of consciousness one is aware of the Self not only within but in everything around one.

In looking at the value of these higher states of consciousness I have so far only considered their effects on individual experience and action. Now in this final section I want to consider the implications of higher states of consciousness for society as a whole, and their significance for the world today. If humanity is to continue to progress it is essential that we develop a deeper awareness of ourselves in relation to the rest of nature. Such a development is, I believe, the next major step in evolution and will form the basis of a healthy and integrated society.

This section is a more personal reflection on the role of the TM program in the world today, and here more than ever any errors or deficiencies must be laid at my door rather than Maharishi's.

The Consciousness Revolution

15

Love the world as yourself
Then you can truly care for all things

Tao-Te-Ching

Humanity is now facing one of the most crucial periods in its history. This no longer needs to be spelt out: any impartial survey of the situation shows that the problems of over-population, resource depletion and pollution are all very real and rapidly getting worse. But this is not going to be another apocalyptic look at the day of doom, nor a hearty reassurance that science and technology alone will see us through – they won't. If we are to avert the coming disaster some very fundamental changes will be necessary: changes in the way that we relate to ourselves, our bodies and our environment; changes in the demands we make of others and of our planet; changes in our awareness, in our thinking and in our appreciation of the world. In short, changes in ourselves.

We still interact with the world on an 'I versus It' basis: 'me-in-here' versus the 'world-out-there'. This distinction stems from the continual need of the unenlightened person to reaffirm his sense of personal identity. The reaffirmation occurs at the expense of the environment – the not-I – and in this respect other people and even our own bodies must be included as part of the environment. We take from the 'out-there' to feed the 'in-here'. This inevitably results in an exploitative consciousness.

Many have placed the blame for our large-scale abuse of ourselves and the environment on our 'consumer society'. But a consumer society is itself reliant upon the needs and desires of unenlightened people. Advertising preys upon an individual's need to bolster his artificial and inadequate self-image. People smoke the 'right' cigarettes, use the 'right' gas, buy clothes with the 'right' label inside not because they are physically any different but because they reinforce a derived sense of identity.

This is not to belittle or ignore the political factors involved. Certainly much of technology and industry is geared towards the short-term ends of a select few. But in many cases those regarded as exploiters are only trying to maintain their own sense of identity. Furthermore they are only able to do this at the expense of others because the others too need to reaffirm their sense of identity – you cannot sell someone a car he does not need physically unless he needs it psychologically.

So the cycle continues. Irreplaceable resources are moulded into objects of temporary support for the ego and then, once their psychological value is spent, thrown away as scrap. Acting in the most short-sighted manner we persist in upsetting the delicate and intricate ecological systems on which we are so dependent. If we were to do this to our own bodies we would surely be certified as insane, but when we do it to our environment it is excused in the name of progress.

The root cause is the fact that we do not really appreciate our essential oneness with the rest of the world. We may know it intellectually, but we do not know it as an immediate awareness, as a personal reality. Our immediate awareness is still one of isolated individual selves, what Alan Watts referred to as 'skin-encapsulated egos'.

On one level this distinction is very real and very necessary, but it is not the whole truth. It is a biologically useful model which develops in early childhood and allows the organism to interact with its immediate environment as an autonomous unit. The model itself is not at fault: the fault lies in having to depend totally upon this dualistic awareness. If as a species we are to advance further it is now imperative that we gain an awareness of our essential oneness with creation to balance this sense of separateness. This awareness must come not merely as a change of idea but as a change of consciousness.

A Paradigm Shift

Thomas Kuhn used the word 'paradigm' to denote the basic theoretical model which underlies the main body of a science, and which serves as a framework for understanding new observations.[1] An example of a paradigm in the field of physics is Newtonian Mechanics. Until the end of the nineteenth century it was possible to explain nearly all that was known about the physical interaction of objects in terms of the principles laid down by Newton in the seventeenth century. But there were a few phenomena which could not be satisfactorily explained by Newton's model. By the beginning of the twentieth century the number had grown to the point where it was no longer possible to accept Newtonian Mechanics as the whole truth and a new paradigm was needed. The new model which emerged was formulated in the Theory of Relativity and this shift has been referred to as the Einsteinian Revolution in physics. Examples of other major paradigm changes in science are the Darwinian Revolution in biology, the Freudian Revolution in psychology, and the Copernican Revolution in astronomy.

It is now becoming increasingly apparent that a paradigm shift is needed in the fields of industry, technology, economics and education. The current model which measures its successes in terms of immediate material returns has become most inappropriate in the present global situation.

Willis Harman and a team of researchers at the Stanford Research Institute made a major study of the possible 'future histories' of mankind and concluded that there were only two alternatives which did not end in collective disaster. The first of these was what was referred to as 'friendly fascism' – 'a managed society which rules by a faceless and widely dispersed complex of warfare–welfare–industrial–communications–police bureaucracies with a technocratic ideology'. This more or less amounts to continuing along present lines into an Orwellian 1984 where stability can only be maintained by force. The second alternative was envisioned as an 'evolutionary transformation'. This, the report summarizes, would (1) entail an ecological ethic; (2) place the highest value on self-development; (3) be multi-valued, multi-faceted and integrative; (4) involve the balancing and co-ordination of satisfactions rather than trying to satisfy just one narrowly defined field (e.g. economic); (5) convey a holistic sense of perspective or understanding of life; and (6) be experimental, open-minded and evolutionary.[2] This amounts to a major paradigm shift in our whole approach to life. The report concluded that such a shift was the only feasible path for humanity.

But however much we may argue for a shift to a new paradigm it is very unlikely to come about while the individuals concerned are themselves still bound to the old 'I versus It' model. We will not be able to build a non-exploitative, holistic, ecological ethic into our policies unless it is also built into our awareness – built in not just in the sense of being understood but as an immediate awareness. We need to know it organically, at the heart of our being, rather than just cerebrally as part of our reasoning. As well as restructuring our model of the world we must restructure the basic model which governs our thinking and experience of the world.

Identity as a Metaparadigm

The models which underlie thinking and experience are paradigms in much the same way as the models which underlie a particular science are. They determine how sensory perception is to be interpreted, which experiences to accept and which to reject as illusion, and in which direction thinking should be channelled.

Different types of mental experience will involve different models. (To make sense of a simple drawing of a cube, for example, requires the tacit assumption that the lines represent a three-dimensional object.) But underlying all experiences there is one fundamental frame of reference which conditions all experience. This is our sense of identity.

The way in which we appreciate ourselves affects not only our experience but also our thinking and the way we act. It is the dominant psychological model which underlies and conditions all mental activity. In this respect it is a mental paradigm. But it is unlike an ordinary paradigm in that it underlies all thinking and not just thinking in one particular field. Moreover it even underlies the generation of paradigms themselves. Since it is something beyond an ordinary paradigm I shall call our sense of identity a *metaparadigm.*

The current metaparadigm is one of an individual self distinct from the rest of the environment. This egocentric model has been very useful both for biological survival, and on a wider scale, for evolutionary progress. Until recently there has been little reason to question it – indeed most Western cultures have strongly supported it. But now that rapidly approaching global crises have forced us to examine the consequences of this model in much greater depth, its fundamental flaws and paradoxical conclusions are becoming increasingly apparent. In this situation a paradigm shift (or rather a metaparadigm shift) is needed. We need to restructure our thinking so as to include our essential unity with the whole of nature as a fundamental element. We need to know not just as an understanding but as an immediate awareness that all aspects of the environment are as much a part of oneself as the body is. It will then become as difficult indiscriminately to cut down a forest or otherwise upset the overall balance of the biosystem as it would to chop off one's own finger.

Gregory Bateson, the anthropologist, psychiatrist and ecologist, has come to very similar conclusions:[3]

> If this ['I versus It' model] is your estimate of your relationship to nature *and you have an advanced technology*, your likelihood of survival will be that of a snowball in hell. You will die either of the toxic by-products of your own hate, or, simply, of over-population and over-grazing. . . .
>
> If I am right, the whole of our thinking about what we are and what other people are has got to be restructured . . . The most important task today is to learn to think in a new way. Let me say that *I* don't know how to think that way. Intellectually I can stand here and I can give you a reasoned exposition of this matter; but if I am cutting down a tree, I still think 'Gregory Bateson' is cutting down the tree. I am cutting down the tree.

But although he comes to the same conclusion as to the type of change necessary, Bateson seems to make the error of expecting an identity between the individual and the outside world. But this experience, although possible is not the same as the experience of union to which I have been referring. In the state of unity consciousness all sense of separation with the outside world is retained.

Added to this is an awareness of the underlying harmony of all creation. The union is not on the level of thought as a unity between an individual self and the rest of creation, but on the level of the Self which underlies both. There is no loss of diversity in enlightenment. So even when Bateson does reach this level of consciousness he will still find that '*I* am cutting down the tree', and added to this there will be the awareness that in essence I and the tree are one. His difficulty is brought out clearly when he says '*I* don't know how to think that way'. He is looking for a unity on the level of thought rather than on the level of Being.

Let me repeat, the structuring of a holistic and ecological consciousness within ourselves does not begin on the level of understanding, nor on the level of the individual ego. It must come from the very center of our being.

A Shift in Metaparadigm

If the change cannot be brought about by merely thinking about it and if the old model is firmly entrenched from childhood onwards, there may seem to be little chance of ever developing an alternative. Some insight into how such a change might occur comes from looking at how ordinary paradigm shifts occur.

Paradigms are built up as the result of experience and retain their status through their continued ability to explain new facts and solve problems within their given field. When the model fails badly a paradigm shift begins and the new paradigm gains status through its ability to account for the observations which could not be accommodated by the old.

The same is true with the metaparadigm. The egocentric, 'I versus It' model is built up during the first two years of life as the child begins to break away from the mother and starts functioning as an autonomous unit. The child begins to experience a duality between itself and the rest of the environment, and builds up a model of the world on this basis. Now the one experience which most shakes this model is the personal experience of a unity with the rest of creation. This cannot be incorporated within the 'I versus It' model and starts a shift towards a new metaparadigm.

It is precisely this experience of unity that the TM program brings about. Comparing the situation with that of a paradigm shift in science we could say that the experiment which brings about the new observation is the process of meditation; the observation which does not fit in with the old model is the experience of oneness found in transcendental consciousness; and the new model which begins to develop, in this case the new metaparadigm, is a higher state of consciousness.

Now the change is by no means immediate. One of the central points of Kuhn's thesis is that paradigm shifts do not happen overnight. Scientists seldom give up their old views of the world without considerable resistance. Throughout scientific history the older generation of scientists have clung rigidly to their models of the world in spite of all the evidence accumulating for the new one. Rather than reject the old paradigm they have frequently preferred to reject the new evidence. A similar phenomenon will undoubtedly occur with a shift in metaparadigm. It is one thing to have experienced one's essential unity with the rest of nature: it is quite another to restructure one's thinking accordingly. People do not easily let go of their presuppositions; their minds adhere to the familiar modes of experience which have served them so well for so long. The change will be gradual and will require the constant repetition of the experience of oneness if this is to coexist along with the equally real experience of diversity. Hence the need for regular daily practice of the TM technique.

Revolution or Evolution

I am not trying to suggest that a general raising of the level of consciousness will by itself cure all our problems. Nor for that matter is Maharishi. All that is being suggested is the general principle that if a large proportion of the population are living in a higher state of consciousness we should be in a better position to find more realistic, co-operative, long-sighted and less selfish answers to the problems now facing mankind. As Maharishi comments:[4]

Although there are certainly many things in the world to be put right, we shall not be able to accomplish this humane ideal by merely reshuffling the environment. It will never humanly succeed until we can see and appreciate that environment at its full value, until we can envision all its possibilities with expanded mind and heart so that they may be actualized to the advantage of everyone and everything in nature.

Some Marxists may doubt whether it is possible for such an approach to bring about a true change in society. 'Social being determines consciousness' is the cry and only by first producing a profound social and political change will the situation be resolved (whether Marx himself took this line is another question). On the other hand, Freud argues that it is the individual's need to repress his lower instincts which is the principal cause of a repressive social structure, i.e. that individual being determines society.[5] The two might seem to be in opposition, but probably they are both right to some extent: the way we are being partly determined by the structure of society and the structure of society being partly determined by the way we are. It's a chicken and egg situation, and you don't break the cycle by getting rid of the chicken because the egg will still hatch, nor by cracking the egg because the chicken will only lay another. Both aspects of the problem have to be treated simultaneously.

The sense in which I have been talking of changing consciousness is different from both the Marxist and the Freudian models. By 'consciousness' or 'self' they are referring to aspects of individual consciousness – and as far as the interaction of the individual self with society is concerned their conclusions may well be correct – but this individual self is not the same as the pure Self, or pure consciousness. The pure Self, by definition, is unconditioned and attributeless. It can neither be changed by the external environment nor does it have any attributes which might condition the external world. In a sense it lies beyond both. But, one effect of gaining an awareness of this pure Self is that perception and thinking both become clearer, and the person with an expanded awareness is in a better position to deal with both the chicken and the egg.

The most radical form of social change is to raise the level of individual consciousness. Political action on its own is incomplete and superficial. The true radicals today are not the extremists: they are those whose concern is the promotion of higher states of consciousness.

Towards a High Synergy Society

The term synergy was coined by Ruth Benedict, the American anthropologist, in 1941.[6] She was studying aggression in various tribal communities and found that societies in which aggression was low or absent had a social structure such that actions which advantaged the individual also advantaged the group as a whole. She called such social orders high synergy societies. Conversely, a low synergy society is one in which an individual while acting for his own good is likely to be acting to the detriment of the group. Such societies tended to be very aggressive.

Since Benedict the term 'synergy' has been extended to many other systems beside societies. The healthy body is a fine example of a high synergy system, the functioning of each cell serving both the needs of the cell and the needs of the body as a whole.

Now the essential point about a high synergy system is that there is no difference between acting for oneself and acting for the good of the whole. Each component of the system may seem to act totally for itself. A muscle cell in your leg, for example, is not concerned at all with the welfare of a cell in the retina of the eye, nor with the welfare of the body as a whole: it has a job to do and gets on with it. But because the healthy organism is a high synergy system the cell is also acting for the good of the whole, which is itself for the good of the cell. Similarly in high synergy societies, the individual is acting for the good of the group not because he is unselfish and puts social obligations before personal desires, but because the good of the individual *is* the good of the group.

Biologically speaking the characteristics of a high synergy system are essentially the characteristics of a healthy organism. This has led several people to consider human societies in terms of organisms. If the parallel holds then it readily becomes apparent that our present social organism is not in a very healthy state. As far as the planet as a whole is concerned many human societies are like giant cancerous growths. Indeed, as Konrad Lorenz points out, there is an astonishing similarity between a picture of a malignant tumour and an aerial photograph of a modern suburb eating its way into the surrounding countryside.[7]

Cancer is a low synergy phenomenon in that individual cells are no longer acting for the good of the body. A malignant cell is one in which the genetic processes are disturbed. The genes control the functioning of each cell and since the same genes are found in every cell of the body they tie the individual cell back to the system as a whole. Without this order the malignant cell no longer performs its proper role in the community but goes off on its own ruthlessly multiplying at the expense of the rest of the organism.

We, the cells of the biosystem, have similarly lost the knowledge of our relationship to the system as a whole. In this case the knowledge resides not in the genes but in the mind. That which is common to all people and which transcends individuality is the experience of oneness, the pure Self. Without this awareness we see ourselves only as isolated 'cells' and go off on our own with almost total disregard for the system as a whole.

In such a low synergy system the individual actions appear to be entirely selfish. But it is not the selfishness which is at fault, the fault lies in our only appreciating ourselves as 'skin-encapsulated egos'. The solution therefore is not to try and subdue our very natural self-interest but to expand our awareness of the self. The enlightened man still acts for the good of himself but since he now appreciates himself and everything else in terms of the universal Self he has gained the awareness which ties him back to the whole and his actions are spontaneously for the good of himself *and* for the good of the whole. This is the beginning of true altruism and an altruism that is not opposed to selfishness. Selfishness and selflessness have become the same. This is the natural and only genuine basis for a high synergy society: a collection of individuals working together not because they are 'do-gooders' but because they are spontaneously in tune with the whole.

Pierre Teilhard de Chardin put forward very similar ideas. He saw two complementary trends in evolution: a tendency towards 'extreme individuation' and a simultaneous tendency towards 'extensive interrelation and co-operation'.[8] In his scheme, evolution is a 'convergence' towards the development of a 'super-consciousness ... a harmonized collectivity of consciousness', in which both trends will reach their full expression: 'the plurality of individual reflections grouping themselves together and reinforcing one another in the act of a single unanimous reflection'.[9] This he sees being brought about by a *megasynthesis* – 'a super-arrangement in which all the thinking elements of the earth find themselves today individually and collectively subject'.[10] But this synthesis will not, he emphasizes, be achieved by any superficial link-ups but by a synthesis of centers: 'it is centre to centre that they must make contact and not otherwise'.[11]

If by center he means the center of consciousness, the pure Self, then this is exactly what Maharishi is saying. We must not try to gain a superficial understanding of our mutual interdependece but a direct personal awareness of our common cores 'so that our individual purposes flow in harmony with all other purposes'.[12]

It is sometimes feared that a society of enlightened men would be a society of sheep. But this is not so. Living for the good of the whole involves no forsaking of individual autonomy and integrity, for, as we have already seen, the experience of unity in no way compromises the experience of diversity: each strengthens the other and both are lived to the full. An 'enlightened' society would be a society of diverse but integrated individuals; a true 'body of people'.

The Force of Evolution

Evolution is a rapidly accelerating process. Each new step occurs in only a fraction of the time that it took for the previous step.

Cosmologists currently put the age of the Universe at around 30,000,000,000 years. This is an incomprehensible stretch of time so in order to get some grasp of it let us imagine it to be contracted into the more familiar period of one year. During the first ten months of that year the earth itself did not exist (it only came into existence some 4,500,000,000 years ago). The first signs of life were single-celled algae and bacteria and these probably appeared about one month ago. About two weeks ago these simple cells began organizing themselves into more complex multi-cellular organisms, but creatures did not start crawling out of the sea until three or four days ago. This was already very late in the history of the planet. Dinosaurs roamed the planet for most of yesterday and during this time the first mammals began to appear. Human beings have been on the scene for about fifteen minutes. Most of this time they have spent as hunters, only beginning to farm the land a few minutes ago. The first civilization did not appear until the last five seconds of the year and our present industrialized-technological society is less than a quarter of a second old. We have only to look at the tremendous advances that have been made in our own lifetimes – a mere few hundredths of a second in that entire year – to see that this rapid acceleration in development shows no signs of abating. What then do the next few thousandths of a second hold in store for us? To see let us go back and look at the pattern behind this evolutionary explosion.

Each major step in evolution has been one of progressive organization and increased complexity. Hydrogen atoms condensed from interstellar space to form the more complex atoms of which our planet is composed. Later, in the 'primordial soup', different atoms became organized into more complex organic molecules, these molecules grouped together to form living cells, and more complex organisms evolved as the individual cells grouped themselves together in more organized systems. Indeed, to be an organism means to have become organized, and the tendency towards increased organization appears to be not only the force behind evolution but the principle of life itself.

If this tendency is to continue it would be tempting to suggest that the next major step in evolution would be a grouping together of individual organisms into well-integrated social units. The trend over the last few thousand years has certainly been in this direction. Over the last two centuries it has been accentuated by the mutual interdependence forced upon us by large-scale industrialization, and more recently technological developments have led to a massive increase in communication between both individuals and groups. Whether this trend results in a state of 'friendly fascism' where the whole world is controlled by a few multi-national industrial corporations, or whether it culminates in a true high synergy society, is up to us. For the first alternative we need do nothing. For the second each individual needs personally to raise his level of awareness and become an active (and conscious) participant in the evolutionary process.

It is impossible to separate the personal development of consciousness from the progressive organization which underlies physical evolution. The two are complementary perspectives of the same process. Consciousness in the mental world is the complement of organization in the physical world. Thus the development of a higher state of consciousness is a manifestation of the 'force of evolution' on the mental level.

This complementary relationship of organization and consciousness might lead one to suggest that some higher degree of organization within social groups would lead to the emergence of a corresponding higher order of consciousness – a social consciousness or group mind. Since this would be the natural counterpart of a high synergy system it would be a social consciousness which was in perfect accord with the consciousness of the individual.

There is a growing scientific interest in what has been called the 'Gaia Hypothesis' – the hypothesis that the planet as a whole behaves very much as a living organism, compensating for atmospheric changes and variations in temperature in such a way as to preserve the optimum conditions for life.[13] If the planet can be thought of as a living organism then society is its nervous system. At this stage in its history, we, the individual cells of society, are making billions of connections with other cells in the system as we develop ever more complex networks of communication. Coupled with this growth in communication on the physical level, an increase in synergy on the mental level would produce the types of coherent patterns of activity across the globe that are at present associated with consciousness in the individual brain. If so we are about to witness the emergence of some form of global consciousness.

Sociologists tend to reject such theories on the grounds that most of the knowledge collected within the social sciences shows no evidence of any such 'group mind'. But this is only to be expected. Although the number of people in the world is the same order of magnitude as the number of neurons in the brain (3.6 thousand million people compared to about ten thousand million neurons) the present degree of organization and interaction between human beings is nothing compared to the incredibly complex and sophisticated network of communications between neurons in the brain. Thus if some group or social mind is in the process of developing it is at present probably comparable to the consciousness of an earthworm and we would hardly expect to be able to detect it. Nevertheless, it may well be that Jung's collective unconscious is the individual manifestation of some rudimentary form of group mind, and that as time goes on we should see the collective unconscious being augmented by a collective consciousness.

Judging from the rate at which evolution has been consistently speeding up, this next step, if it occurs, will come in the next decade or two. This would be what Teilhard de Chardin referred to as the *Omega Point*: the point where 'the Universal and the Personal ... culminate in each other'.[14] Maharishi is more precise about the timing. He maintains that the transition to a new age, what he calls the 'Age of Enlightenment', began early in 1975. As from this date there was a sufficient number of people moving forward into higher states of consciousness to carry the rest of the population with them. And he predicted that as more and more people reached enlightenment the effect would become noticeable throughout society.

To many the idea that we are now moving into an Age of Enlightenment appears highly fanciful. Suffering, conflict and unrest are all around us, and seem far more dominating than any harmonious influences there might be. What Maharishi is saying, however, is not that we are now living the full value of such a new age, but that the shift has begun, we are now moving in that direction. He calls the present time the *Dawn* of the Age of Enlightenment, and the dawn always begins at the darkest hour of the night.

A Sociological Phase Transition

This may all sound highly optimistic; looking at the rapidly approaching global crises there would seem to be very little chance of humanity surviving long enough to see the transition through. Certainly the threat is very great and the vast majority of people still support the egocentric-exploitative models which are leading straight to their own destruction. Yet with many other transitions in nature there is often no inkling of the coming change until the transition occurs. Take the case of boiling water, for example. As the water begins to heat up a few but increasing number of molecules escape to form water vapour. As the water is heated up further the number of molecules escaping gradually increases until, at the boiling point, there is a sudden change in which the molecules boil off very rapidly and restructure themselves as a gas. There is said to have been a phase transition from water to steam. It is possible that as more and more individuals move into higher states of consciousness society will reach a point at which it undergoes a similar phase transition – a 'sociological phase transition'. But if so there would be little overall sign of the coming change until it actually occurred. The old trends would dominate right up to the transition point just as water remains water from 1°C right up to 99°C.

Maharishi sees this phase transition in terms of a spread of orderliness and coherence throughout society, and it will come, he says, as the result of a spread of growth and orderliness within the individual. Drawing a parallel with coherent phenomena in physics, Dr Lawrence Domash, a professor of physics at MIU, has pointed out that only a small proportion of the elements in a system need to display coherence for the effect to be felt throughout the whole.[15] Whereas random fluctuations largely tend to cancel each other out, coherent activities tend to add up and soon become noticeable. Calculations from physical phenomena such as coherent light generation (i.e. lasers) show that if the number of elements in a system is 'n' then the number of elements that need to be functioning coherently for the effect to begin to become noticeable is of the order of the square root of 'n'. (I have already looked at how this accounts for the emergence of individual consciousness from a brain in Chapter 3.) Domash applies this to a society in which some of the population practise the TM technique, on the assumption that during the technique the increased coherence of brain wave activity is having a similar ordering effect on other individuals (and there is now growing evidence that this is occurring). He allows for the fact that people are only practising the TM technique for a small fraction of the day by multiplying a factor of 50 – presumably if the individuals in question were enlightened this would not be necessary – and comes up with a figure of $50/\sqrt{n}$ for the fraction of the population that need to be practising the TM technique for the social effect to be noticeable. For a country the size of the United States this fraction is about $\frac{1}{4}$ per cent, and for England it is about 1 per cent. These figures, it is argued, represent the threshold for a 'sociological phase transition'.

Recent studies suggest that this idea is not quite so far-fetched as it might at first appear. There are now quite a few cities in the United States in which the number of people practising the TM technique has exceeded this theoretical threshold. Looking at the official crime rate statistics for these cities it has been found that there was a decrease of 8.8 per cent, and this at a time when for the nation as a whole the crime rate in cities was increasing at six per cent per year. There was also found to be a significant correlation between the proportion of people practising the TM technique in each city and the specific decrease in crime rate in that city.[16] Any study of this kind must of course be viewed with caution. There are inevitably many uncontrolled variables which make it difficult to prove any cause–effect relationship. Nevertheless the results were remarkably consistent over many cities, and, if further research bears them out, they offer some support for Maharishi's claim that if only a small percentage of the world practised the TM technique the course of history would be changed.

Alpha or Omega?

Kenneth Boulding, the economist and futurist, writes that 'the twentieth century marks the middle period of a great transition in the state of the human race. It may properly be called the second great transition in the history of mankind.'[17] And John R. Platt comments that 'the act of saving ourselves, if it succeeds, will make us participants in the most incredible event in evolution.'[18] But whether we rise to the challenge and move on, through the omega point, to a new era of evolution, or whether civilization as we now know it extinguishes itself as some evolutionary blind alley is up to us.

If the challenge is met we will pass through a major cultural revolution – a Revolution of Consciousness. And a revolution to which the Industrial Revolution, the Russian Revolution and the Einsteinian Revolution were only prologues.

In the true sense of the word revolution the Self will return to take its rightful place at the center of consciousness just as in the Copernican Revolution the sun resumed its rightful place at the center of the solar system. But the Copernican Revolution did not come about by destroying the falsely placed earth or holding the sun still, and the Revolution of Consciousness will not come about by destroying the falsely placed ego or holding on to an idea of the Self: it will only come as a result of personal experience. Thinking about it, writing about it, talking about it will not by themselves produce the necessary changes in consciousness. In this respect the present book, or any other book for that matter, can be of little help. It is only more words about that which is essentially beyond words.

The evolution of consciousness must move out of the speculative, philosophical realm and into the empirical. And when I say 'must' I do not mean it as a logical necessity – it could well not happen – but as a cosmic imperative. If we delay a hundred or even fifty years it will almost certainly be too late.

Every major step in evolution has been built upon the foundations laid down by the previous changes. The last major change was the emergence of individual self-awareness in which man became conscious of himself as a thinking being. He thereby gained the ability to make conscious decisions about his own future. This must now become the basis for the next step. Thus the fundamental difference between the coming step and all previous ones is that we, and this means each and every one of us, are now responsible for seeing the process through.

But just the ability to choose is not enough. We cannot make decisions without a knowledge of what is possible. We need an image of the future, a vision of possibilities, to draw us on in the right direction, and some means to make this image an actuality. Here I can do no more than point a direction and suggest a path. In this respect the present book may serve as a first step. The next step, however, is up to you.

Principal Centers for the TM Program

Appendix

USA

Atlanta
3615 North Stratford
Road NE
Atlanta, GA 30342

Berkeley
2716 Derby Street
Berkeley, CA 94705
(415) 548-1144

Boston
73 Newbury Street
Boston, MA 02116

Cambridge
33 Garden Street
Cambridge, MA 02138
(617) 876-4581

Charlotte
1532 E. Morehead Street
Charlotte, NC 28207

Chicago
145 E. Ohio corner of
N. Michigan
Chicago, ILL 60611
(312) 467-5570

Cincinnati
3047 Madison Road
Cincinnati, OH 45209

Colombus
1818 W. Lane Ave
Colombus, OH 43221

Denver
215 St Paul
Suite 280
Denver, CO 80206

Des Moines
1311 34th Street
Des Moines, IA 50311

Detroit
17108 Mack at Cadieux
Grosse point, MI 48230
Hartford
299 Farmington Ave
Hartford, CT 06105
Honolulu
227 S. King Street
Honolulu, HI 96813
Houston
2518 Drexel
Houston, TX 77207
Kansas City
6301 Main Street
Kansas City, MO 64113
Los Angeles
1015 Gayley Ave
Los Angeles, CA 90024
(213) 478-1569
Miami
3251 Ponce de Leon
Suite 210
Coral Gables, FL 33134
Milwaukee
40 E. Silver Spring
Whitefish Bay, WI 53217
Minneapolis
6524 Walker St. No. 212
St Louis Park, MO 55426
New Haven
1974 Yale Station
New Haven, CT 06520
New York
133 E. 58th Street
14th Floor
New York, NY 10022
(212) 826 6620
Philadelphia
315 S. 17th Street
Philadelphia, PA 19103
(215) 732-9220

Pittsburgh
5883 Forbes Ave
Pittsburgh, PA 15217
Portland
7743 S.W. Capitol Highway
Portland, OR 97219
Sacramento
2454 Loma Vista Drive
Sacramento, CA 95825
St Louis
742 Emerson Road
St Louis, MO 63141
San Francisco
256 Laguna Honda Blvd
San Francisco, CA 94116
Seattle
912 15th Ave
Seattle, WA 98112
(206) 322-1800
Washington D.C.
2127 Leroy Place N.W.
Washington D.C. 20008
(202) 387-5050

CANADA

Calgary
218-11th Ave S.W.
Calgary, Alberta
(403) 269-6781
Edmonton
Le Marchand Mansions
101-11523-100th Ave
Edmonton, Alberta
(403) 488-0148
Halifax
2045 Poplar St
Halifax, Nova Scotia
(902) 422-5905

Hamilton
1960 Main St
Hamilton, Ontario
(416) 527-0444

Montreal
3666 Lorne Crescent
Montreal, P.Q.
(514) 285-1298

Ottawa
65 Bank St
4th Floor
Ottawa, Ontario, K1P 5N2
(613) 232-2671

Quebec
1085 Ave des Erables
Quebec City, P.Q., G1R 2N3
(418) 529-2149

Regina
2326 Albert St
Regina, Saskatchewan,
S4P 2V7
(306) 586-4012

Saskatoon
707 University Dr
Saskatoon, Saskatchewan,
S7N PJ3
(306) 242-6317

Toronto
250 Merton St
Toronto, Ontario, M4S 1B1
(416) 482-5440

Vancouver
1170 Hornby St E.
Vancouver, B.C., V6Z 1O8
(604) 688-4528

Victoria
1270 Pandora Ave
Victoria, B.C., V8V 3R4
(604) 383-9822

Winnipeg
51 Horace St
Winnipeg, Manitoba,
R2H 0V8
(204) 247-5565

Chapter 3: The Nature of the Mind

1. Maharishi Mahesh Yogi, *The Science of Being and Art of Living*, SRM Publications, London, 1966, p.54.
2. Peter Russell, 'Transcendental meditation and conscious experience', paper presented at Brain Research Association Conference on Transcendental Meditation, Exeter, 1973.
3. Maharishi Mahesh Yogi, *Bhagavad-Gita, A New Translation and Commentary, Chapters 1-6,* Penguin Books, London, 1966, p. 470.
4. Idries Shah, *The Exploits of the Incomparable Mulla Nasrudin*, Dutton, New York, 1972, pp.26-7.

Chapter 4: The TM Technique

1. Quoted in William James, *The Varieties of Religious Experience*, Fontana, London, 1960, p.385.
2. Anonymous, *The Cloud of Unknowing*, transl. C. Wolter, Penguin Books, London, 1961, ch. 52.
3. Maharishi Mahesh Yogi, *Bhagavad-Gita, A New Translation and Commentary, Chapters 1-6,* Penguin Books, London, 1966, p.470.
4. Lyle Watson, *Supernature*, Hodder & Stoughton, London, 1973, pp.105-7.

5. E. Bryhni, A. Fjeld and A. Løvlie, 'Mechanical shocks induce phenocopies of developmental mutants', *Nature*, vol. 248, pp.794-5.
6. Roberto Assagioli, *Psychosynthesis*, Viking, New York, 1965, pp.237-66.
7. Hans Jenny, *Kymatics*, Basilius Press, Basle, 1967.
8. Shankara, *The Crest Jewel Of Discrimination*, Advaita Ashram, Almora, India, 1970, p.22.
9. Maharishi Mahesh Yogi, *The Science of Being and Art of Living*, SRM Publications, London, 1966, pp.58, 59.

Chapter 5: TM Research

1. John Allison, 'Respiratory changes during Transcendental Meditation', *Lancet*, 1970, vol. i, p.833.
2. R. Keith Wallace and Herbert Benson, 'The physiology of meditation', *Scientific American*, vol. 226, no. 2, pp.84-90.
3. John T. Farrow, 'Physiological changes associated with transcendental consciousness, the state of least excitation of consciousness', in Orme-Johnson and Farrow, below.
4. J. Russell Herbert, 'Periodic suspension of respiration during the Transcendental Meditation technique', in Orme-Johnson and Farrow, below.
5. Robert R. Pagano, Richard M. Rose, Robert M. Stivers, and Stephen Warrenburg, 'Sleep during Transcendental Meditation', *Science*, vol. 191, pp. 308-9.
6. R. Keith Wallace, 'Physiological effects of Transcendental Meditation', *Science*, vol. 167, pp.1751-4.
7. Farrow, op. cit.
8. R. Keith Wallace, 'The physiological effects of Transcendental Meditation: a proposed fourth major state of consciousness', Ph.D. thesis, Department of Physiology, University of Calif., 1970.
9. Herbert Benson and R. Keith Wallace, 'Decreased blood pressure in hypertensive subjects who practised meditation', *Circulation*, vols 45 and 46, supplement II.
10. Tom J. Routt, 'Low normal heart and respiratory rates in practitioners of Transcendental Meditation', in Orme-Johnson and Farrow, below; and Benson and Wallace, op. cit.
11. Wallace and Benson, op. cit. and R. Keith Wallace, Herbert Benson and Archie F. Wilson, 'A wakeful hypometabolic physiologic state', *American Journal of Physiology*, vol. 221, no. 3, pp.795-9.
12. R. Jevning, A. Wilson, E. VanderLaan and S. Lavine, 'Plasma Prolactin and Cortisol during Transcendental Meditation', in Orme-Johnson and Farrow, below.
13. Wallace, Benson and Wilson, op. cit.; and David W. Orme-Johnson, 'Autonomic stability and Transcendental Meditation', *Psychosomatic Medicine*, vol. 35, no. 4, pp.341-9.

14. David W. Orme-Johnson and John T. Farrow, *Scientific Research on Transcendental Meditation: Collected Papers,* vol. 1, MIU Press, New York, 1975.
15. Elmer E. Green and Alyce M. Green, 'Volition as a metaforce in psychophysiological self-regulation', paper delivered at Sixth Annual Medical Meeting of the Association for Research and Enlightenment, Phoenix, Arizona, 1973.
16. Herbert Benson, *The Relaxation Response*, William Morrow, New York, 1975.
17. See Philip Goldberg, *'The TM Program'*, Holt, Rinehart & Winston, New York, 1976, p.75.
18. Wallace, Benson and Wilson, op. cit.
19. Robert E. Ornstein, *The Psychology of Consciousness,* W. H. Freeman, San Francisco, 1972.
20. Gillian Cohen, 'Hemispheric differences in serial versus parallel processing', *Journal of Experimental Psychology,* vol. 97, no. 3, pp.349-56.
21. Bernard Glueck, 'Biofeedback and meditation in the treatment of psychiatric illness', *Comprehensive Psychiatry,* vol. 16, no. 4, p.310.
22. J.-P. Banquet, 'Spectral analysis of the EEG during meditation', *Electroencephalography and Clinical Neurophysiology,* vol. 35, pp.143-51.
23. Paul H. Levine, J. Russell Herbert, Christopher T. Haynes, and Urs Strobel, 'EEG Coherence during the Transcendental Meditation technique', in Orme-Johnson and Farrow, op. cit.
24. Farrow, op. cit.
25. Mark Westcott, 'Hemispheric symmetry of the EEG during Transcendental Meditation', in Orme-Johnson and Farrow, op. cit.

Chapter 6: The Relief of Stress

1. Peter Blythe, *Stress Disease,* Arthur Barker, London, 1973, pp.17-19.
2. Lennart Levi, *Stress and Distress in Response to Psychosocial Stimuli,* Pergamon, London, 1973.
3. Una Kroll, *The Healing Potential of Transcendental Meditation,* John Knox Press, Atlanta, 1974.
4. David W. Orme-Johnson, 'Autonomic stability and Transcendental Meditation', *Psychosomatic Medicine,* vol. 35, no. 4, pp.341-9.
5. Denver Daniels, personal communication.

Chapter 7: Health, Creativity and Intelligence

1. Elmer E. Green, *The May Lectures,* Brunel College, London, 1974.
2. See Peter Blythe, *Stress Disease,* Arthur Barker, London, 1973, pp. 34 and 62; and O. Carl Simonton, and Stephanie S. Simonton, 'Belief systems and management of the emotional aspects of malignancy', *Journal of Transpersonal Psychology,* vol. 7, pp.29-47.

References

3. Frank Papentin, 'Self-purification of the organism and Transcendental Meditation', in David W. Orme-Johnson and John T. Farrow, *Scientific Research on Transcendental Meditation; Collected Papers,* vol. 1, MIU Press, New York, 1975.
4. Quoted in *The Psychology of Transcendental Meditation: A Literature Review,* eds Demetri P. Kanellakos and Jerome S. Lukas, W. A. Benjamin, Menlo Park, Calif., 1975, p.132.
5. Bernard C. Glueck, and Charles F. Stroebel, 'Biofeedback and meditation in the treatment of psychiatric illnesses', *Comprehensive Psychiatry,* vol. 16, pp.303-21.
6. Harold Bloomfield, Michael Cain and Dennis Jaffe, *TM: Discovering Inner Energy and Overcoming Stress,* Delacorte, New York, 1975.
7. Harold Bloomfield, 'Some observations on the uses of the Transcendental Meditation program in psychiatry', in Orme-Johnson and Farrow, op. cit.
8. Daniel Goleman, 'Meditation as meta-therapy: hypotheses toward a proposed fifth state of consciousness', *Journal of Transpersonal Psychology,* vol. 3, pp.14, 15.
9. John Graham, 'Auditory discrimination in meditators', in Orme-Johnson and Farrow, op. cit.
10. Michael Pirot, 'Transcendental Meditation and perceptual auditory discrimination', in Orme-Johnson and Farrow, op. cit.
11. Frederick M. Brown, *et al.,* 'EEG kappa rhythms during Transcendental Meditation and possible perceptual threshold changes following', paper presented at the Kentucky Academy of Science, USA, November 1971.
12. Robert Shaw and David Kolb, 'One-point reaction time involving meditators and non-meditators', in Orme-Johnson and Farrow, op. cit.
13. Karen Blasdell, 'The effects of Transcendental Meditation upon a complex perceptual motor task', in Orme-Johnson and Farrow, op. cit.
14. Peter Russell, 'Transcendental meditation and conscious experience', paper presented at Brain Research Association Conference on Transcendental Meditation, Exeter, 1973.
15. André S. Tjoa, 'Some evidence that the practice of Transcendental Meditation increases intelligence as measured by a psychological test', in Orme-Johnson and Farrow, op. cit.
16. Maharishi Mahesh Yogi, *Maharishi International University Catalogue,* MIU Press, Los Angeles and Seelisberg, Switzerland, 1974, p.37.
17. Erwin Schrödinger, *What is Life?,* Cambridge University Press, London, 1969, p.78.
18. Michael J. MacCullum, 'Transcendental Meditation and creativity', in Orme-Johnson and Farrow, op. cit.; and Howard Shecter, 'The Transcendental Meditation program in the classroom: a psychological evaluation of the science of creative intelligence', ibid.
19. Christopher T. Haynes, J. Russell Herbert, William Reber, David W. Orme-Johnson, 'The psychophysiology of advanced participants in

the Transcendental Meditation program: Correlations of EEG coherence, creativity, H-reflex recovery, and experience of transcendental consciousness', in Orme-Johnson and Farrow, op. cit.

Chapter 8: The Fourth State of Consciousness

1. Peter Russell and Alistair Shearer, *The Upanishads*, Wildwood House, London, 1977.
2. Quoted in Walter T. Stace, *Mysticisim and Philosophy*, Macmillan, London, 1961, p.104.
3. Quoted in J. E. Coleman, *The Quiet Mind*, Rider, London, 1971, pp.83, 87.
4. Quoted in Una Kroll, *The Healing Potential of Transcendental Meditation*, John Knox Press, Atlanta, 1974, pp.103-4.
5. Quoted in Stace, op. cit., p.87.
6. Quoted in Abraham Maslow, *The Farther Reaches of Human Nature*, Penguin Books, London, 1973, p.194.
7. Swami Prabhavanda and Frederick Manchester, *The Upanishads*, Mentor, New York, 1957, p.21.
8. Aldous Huxley, *The Perennial Philosophy*, Fontana, London, 1958, pp.17-18.

Chapter 10: Self-Realization

1. Maharishi Mahesh Yogi, *Bhagavad-Gita, A New Translation and Commentary, Chapters 1-6*, Penguin Books, London, 1966, p.142.
2. Quoted in Jack Forem, *Transcendental Meditation*, Dutton, New York, 1973, p.183.
3. Sidney Spencer, *Mysticism in World Religion*, Penguin Books, London, 1963, pp.72-5.
4. See Maharishi, op. cit., p.282.
5. Lao-Tsu, *Tao-Te-Ching*, transl. Jane English and Gia-Fu Feng, Knopf, New York, 1972, ch. 15.

Chapter 11: Higher States of Consciousness

1. John Sinclair (transl.), *The Divine Comedy of Dante Alighieri*, vol. 3, John Lane The Bodley Head, London, 1946.
2. Quoted in Evelyn Underhill, *Mysticism*, Dutton, New York, 1961, p.251.
3. Walt Whitman, *Leaves of Grass*, McKay, 1891, p.323.
4. Quoted in Rudolph Otto, *Mysticism, East and West*, Macmillan, New York, 1932, p.61.
5. Maharishi Mahesh Yogi, *The Science of Being and Art of Living*, SRM Publications, London, 1966, p.250.

6. Sidney Spencer, *Mysticism in World Religion*, Penguin Books, London, 1963, p.9.
7. F. C. Happold, *Mysticism: A Study and an Anthology*, Penguin Books, London, 1963, p.351.
8. Lao-Tsu, *Tao-Te-Ching*, transl. Jane English and Gia-Fu Feng, Knopf, New York, 1972, ch. 38.
9. Maharishi Mahesh Yogi, *Bhagavad-Gita, A New Translation and Commentary, Chapters 1-6*, Penguin Books, London, 1966, pp.12-17.

Chapter 12: Some Psychological Perspectives

1. Abraham Maslow, *Toward a Psychology of Being*, Van Nostrand, Reinhold, New York, 1968, p.25.
2. W. Seeman, S. Nidich and T. Banta, 'The influence of Transcendental Meditation on a measure of self-actualisation', *Journal of Counseling Psychology*, vol. 19, no. 3, pp.184-7.
3. W. Seeman, S. Nidich and T. Dreskin, 'Influence of Transcendental Meditation: a replication', *Journal of Counseling Psychology*, vol. 20, no. 6, pp.555-6; and Philip C. Ferguson and John C. Gowan, 'The influence of Transcendental Meditation on anxiety, depression, aggression, neuroticism and self-actualisation', paper presented at California State Psychological Association, Fresno, Calif., January 1974.
4. Ibid.
5. William P. Van den Berg and Bert Mulder, 'Psychological research on the effects of Transcendental Meditation on a number of personality variables using the NPI', in Orme-Johnson and Farrow, *Scientific Research on Transcendental Meditation: Collected Papers*, vol. 1, MIU Press, New York, 1975; and Theo Fehr *et al.*, 'Study of 49 practitioners of Transcendental Meditation with the Freiburger Personality Inventory', in Orme-Johnson and Farrow, op. cit.
6. Lawrence Farwell, 'Effect of Transcendental Meditation on level of anxiety', in Orme-Johnson and Farrow, op. cit.; Ferguson and Gowan, op. cit.; and Larry A. Rjelle, 'Transcendental Meditation and psychological health', in Orme-Johnson and Farrow, op. cit.
7. Colin Wilson, *New Pathways in Psychology*, Gollancz, London, 1972, p.16.
8. Abraham Maslow, *Religions, Values and Peak-Experiences*, Viking, New York, 1970 (new introduction).
9. Daniel Goleman, 'Meditation as meta-therapy: hypotheses toward a proposed fifth state of consciousness', *Journal of Transpersonal Psychology*, vol. 3, p.4.
10. *Journal of Transpersonal Psychology*, Statement of Purpose.
11. Roberto Assagioli, *Psychosynthesis*, Viking, New York, 1965, p.18.
12. Herbert Benson, R. Keith Wallace, *et al.*, 'Decreased drug abuse with Transcendental Meditation – A study of 1,862 subjects', International Conference on Drug-Abuse Problems, Ann Arbor, Michigan, November 1970.

13. Eva Brautigam, *Effect of Transcendental Meditation on Drug Abusers*, Malmö, Sweden; W. Thomas Winquist and G. T. Slatin, 'The effect of Transcendental Meditation on students involved in the regular use of hallucinogenic and "hard drugs" ' and Otis, 'Reduced use of non-prescribed drugs', Stanford Research Institute, 1972 (copies of these papers available from SIMS, Los Angeles); and M. Shafii, R. Lavely and R. Jaffe, 'Meditation and Marihuana', *American Journal of Psychiatry*, vol. 131.1, pp.60-3.
14. Winquist and Slatin, op. cit.

Chapter 13: The Means and the Ends

1. Ram Dass, Lecture at the Maryland Psychiatric Research Center, reprinted in *Journal of Transpersonal Psychology*, vol. 2, p.194.
2. Roberto Assagioli, *The Balancing and Synthesis of Opposites*, Psychosynthesis Research Foundation, New York, 1972.
3. Christmas Humphreys, *Basic Buddhism*, Buddhist Society, London, 1963, p.10.

Chapter 14: The Knower and the Known

1. Alvin Toffler, *Future Shock*, Pan, London, 1971, p.371.
2. A. N. Whitehead, *The Aims of Education*, Ernest Benn, London, 1950, p.1.
3. Quoted in Paul Goodman, *Compulsory Miseducation*, Penguin Books, London, 1971, p.9.
4. Aldous Huxley, *The Perennial Philosophy*, Fontana, London, 1958, p.9.
5. Aldous Huxley, *The Doors of Perception*, Penguin Books, London, 1959, pp.60-5.
6. *Maharishi International University Catalogue* (1st edition), MIU Press, Seelisberg, Switzerland, 1974, p.9.
7. Roy W. Collier, 'The effect of Transcendental Meditation upon university academic attainment', *Proceedings of the Pacific Northwest Conference on Foreign Languages*, Seattle, Washington (in press); and Dennis P. Heaton and David W. Orme-Johnson, 'Influence of Transcendental Meditation on grade point average: initial findings', in Orme-Johnson and Farrow, *Scientific Research on Transcendental Meditation: Collected Papers*, vol. 1, MIU Press, New York, 1975.
8. *Maharishi International University Catalogue* (2nd edition), p.4.
9. Ibid., p.14.

Chapter 15: The Consciousness Revolution

1. Thomas Kuhn, *The Structure of Scientific Revolutions*, University of Chicago Press, 1970.

References

2. Willis Harman *et al.*, 'Changing Images of Man', Stanford Research Institute Center for the Study of Social Policy, Policy Research Report no. 4, 1974.
3. Gregory Bateson, *Steps to an Ecology of Mind*, Paladin, London, 1973, p.437.
4. Maharishi Mahesh Yogi, *Creative Intelligence*, journal published by SRM, London, no. 3, p.2.
5. Sigmund Freud, *Civilisation and Its Discontents*, Hogarth, London, 1930.
6. Quoted in Abraham Maslow, *The Farther Reaches of Human Nature*, Penguin Books, London, 1973, p.210.
7. Konrad Lorenz, *Civilised Man's Eight Deadly Sins*, Methuen, London, 1974.
8. Pierre Teilhard de Chardin, *The Phenomenon of Man*, Fontana, London, 1965, p.21.
9. Ibid., pp.27, 277.
10. Ibid., p.268.
11. Ibid., p.290.
12. Maharishi, loc. cit.
13. James Lovelock, Sidney Epton, 'The quest for Gaia', *New Scientist*, 6 February 1975, pp.304-6.
14. Teilhard de Chardin, op. cit., p.285.
15. Lawrence Domash, MIU video tape: 'Solution'.
16. Garland Landrith and Candace Borland, 'Improved Quality of City Life: Decreased Crime Rate', in Orme-Johnson and Farrow, *Transcendental Meditation: Collected Papers*, vol. 1, MIU Press, New York, 1975.
17. Kenneth E. Boulding, *The Meaning of the Twentieth Century: The Great Transition*, Harper & Row, New York, 1964, p.1.
18. John R. Platt, 'The step to man', *Science*, vol. 149, p.607.

Index

Absolute (and relative), 93ff.; awareness of, 117-21, 143
Academic performance, 154
Action, right, 112-14, 146; as effect not cause of enlightenment, 140, 142
Action-impression-desire, cycle of, 103ff.
Activity, value in developing fifth state of consciousness, 100-1
Age of Enlightenment, *see* Enlightenment, Age of
Alchemy, 144-5
Alice, 27-8
Allison, John, 42-3
Alpha-waves, 51-2
Altruism, and selfishness, 168
Assagioli, Roberto, 36, 132-3; and synthesis of opposites, 143-4
Attachment, 109-10

Banquet, Jean-Paul, 54-5
Bateson, Gregory, 163-4

Being, pure, 93, 99
Belief, lack of, in the TM program, 34, 124
Benedict, Ruth, 166-7
Benson, Herbert, 50-1
Bhagavad-Gita, 109, 126
Bhakti Yoga, 141-2
Biofeedback, 48-9; and treatment of schizophrenia, 71
Blake, William, 115, 117
Blasdell, Karen, 76
Blood: chemistry, 47; pressure, 47
Bloomfield, Harold, 71-2
Blythe, Peter, 70
Bohr, Neils, 106
Boulding, Kenneth, 174
Brahman, 38
Brahmananda Saraswati, 10-12
Brain: left and right hemispheres, 52-4, 57-8, 77, 79; -waves, coherence, 55-6; *see also* Mind
Breathing changes, 41-6, 55; imitation of, 44, 141

6719082

SOME RELATED BOOKS

*The Life of Buddha as Legend and History
Edward J. Thomas

*The Mystics of Islam
R. A. Nicholson

The Visits of the Queen of Sheba
Miguel Serrano

The I Ching and Mankind
Diana ffarington Hook

The I Ching and You
Diana ffarington Hook

Zen in the Art of Helping
David Brandon

*Zen in the Art of Flower Arrangement
An Introduction to the Spirit of the Japanese Art of Flower Arrangement
Gustie L. Herrigel
Foreword by D. T. Suzuki

*Beyond the Body
The Human Double and the Astral Plane
Benjamin Walker

*Ghost and Ghoul
T. C. Lethbridge

*Also available in paperback

ROUTLEDGE & KEGAN PAUL

THE TM TECHNIQUE

This clear and authoritative explanation by a scientist who is also a leading TM teacher is the key to a complete understanding of the Transcendental Meditation technique. Now being translated into five foreign languages, Peter Russell's book has rapidly become recognized as the most profound and comprehensive TM book yet published. It is now available in the United States in this new revised edition.

As well as providing an excellent introduction to the TM program, the book makes a probing investigation of the practice itself and the teachings of Maharishi Mahesh Yogi on the subject, dealing with many of the questions that other books have left unanswered. Peter Russell shows how and why the TM technique works, gives a critical evaluation of the latest scientific research on the practice, and examines the benefits claimed for it. The second part of the book gives an in depth analysis of Maharishi's teachings on higher states of consciousness, looking at what such states represent, how they develop, and how one's awareness of the world changes as a result. The author goes on to discuss recent developments in psychology which give a closer understanding of these states, their significance in education, and the way in which they furnish a synthesis of Eastern and Western thinking.

The last section of the book deals with the role of the TM program in the world today, showing how an expansion of awareness in the individual will lead to the emergence of a healthier, more integrated society. This, Peter Russell suggests, will represent the next major step in the whole pattern of evolution, and in showing what such a new age will mean for the world, he offers some fascinating new perspectives on the Age of Enlightenment.

'This is a clear and concise explanation of the TM program. It investigates many interesting aspects of the subject and can be confidently recommended to anyone wanting to know more about the TM technique and its background.' — ANTHONY CAMPBELL, author of *The Seven States of Consciousness* and *The Mechanics of Enlightenment*

The Author
Peter Russell studied mathematics and theoretical physics at the University of Cambridge, England, turning to psychology as he became fascinated by the subject of consciousness and the untapped potentials of the human mind. He later took a post-graduate degree in Computer Science, also at Cambridge. He studied in India under Maharishi, and trained there as a teacher of the TM technique. He worked further with Maharishi in Europe and America, and has spent three years at the University of Bristol researching into the TM program. Peter Russell has been a TM teacher for seven years and has run many residential courses on the subject. He has lectured widely and has appeared frequently on radio and TV.

ISBN 0 7100 8672 5